Preliminary Materials For a

Theory of the Young-Girl

SEMIOTEXT(E) INTERVENTION SERIES

Published by Semiotext(e)
PO Box 629, South Pasadena, CA 91031
www.semiotexte.com

Thanks to Robert Dewhurst, John Ebert, Joshua Jordan,
John Kelsey, Jason Smith, Sarah Wang and Noura Wedell.

Design: Hedi El Kholti

ISBN: 978-1-58435-108-5
Distributed by The MIT Press, Cambridge, Mass.
and London, England
Printed in the United States of America

10 9 8 7 6

Tiqqun

————

Preliminary Materials For a

Theory of the Young-Girl

Translated by Ariana Reines

semiotext(e)
intervention
series □ 12

Contents

— I did love you once.
Hamlet

PRELIMINARIES

I

Behind the hypnotic grimace of official pacification there is a war being waged. A war that can no longer merely be called economic, social, or humanitarian. It has become *total*. Although everyone senses that their existence has become a battlefield upon which neuroses, phobias, somatizations, depression, and anxiety each sound a retreat, nobody has yet really grasped what is happening or what is at stake. Paradoxically, it is the total nature of this war—total in its means no less than its ends—that has allowed it to remain invisible.

Rather than open offensives, Empire prefers more intricate methods, chronic preventative measures, the molecular diffusion of constraint into everyday life. Here, internal police conveniently takes over for general policing, individual self-control for social control. Ultimately, it's the omnipresence of the new police that has made the war undetectable.

II

What is at stake in the current war are forms-of-life, which is to say, for Empire, their selection, management, and attenuation. The stranglehold of Spectacle over the public expression of desires, the biopolitical monopoly on all medical power-knowledge, the restraints placed on all deviance by an army ever better-equipped with psychiatrists, coaches, and other benevolent "facilitators," the aesthetico-police *booking* of each individual according to her/his biological determinations, the ever more imperative and detailed surveillance of behavior, the proscription by common accord against "violence," all this enters into the anthropological project, or rather the anthropo*technical* project of Empire. *It is a matter of profiling citizens*.

Evidently, impeding the expression of forms-of-life—forms-of-life not as something that would mold a material from the outside, material that would otherwise remain formless, "bare life," but rather as that which affects every body-in-situation with a certain tendency, an intimate motion—does not result from a pure politics of repression. A whole imperial project of diversion, interference, and polarization of bodies centered on absences and impossibilities is at work. The impact is less immediate but also more durable. Over time, and via so many combined effects, THEY ultimately obtain the desired disarmament—in particular *immuno*-disarmament—of bodies.

The vanquished in this war are not so much citizens as those who, denying its reality, have capitulated from the outset: what THEY allow the vanquished, in the guise of "existence," is now nothing but a *lifelong* struggle to render oneself compatible with Empire. But for the others, for us, every gesture, every desire, every affect encounters, at some distance, the need to annihilate Empire and its citizens. A question of letting passions breathe in their fullness. Following this criminal path, we have the time; nothing obliges us to seek out direct confrontation. That would be proof of weakness. Assaults will be launched, however, assaults which will be less important than the *position* from which they originate, for our assaults undermine Empire's forces just as our position undermines its strategy. Accordingly, the more Empire will seem to be accumulating victories, the deeper it will bury itself in defeat, and the more irremediable the defeat will be. Imperial strategy consists first of organizing the blindness of forms-of-life and their illiteracy when it comes to ethical differences, of rendering the battlefield difficult to distinguish if not invisible, and in the most critical cases, of masking the *real war* in all manner of false conflicts.

Retaking the offensive for our side is a matter of making the battlefield manifest. The figure of the Young-Girl is a *vision machine* conceived to this effect. Some will use it to account for the massive character of hostile occupation forces in our existences, others, more vigorous, will use it to determine the speed and direction of their advance. What each of us does with this vision machine will show what we're worth.

III

Listen: The Young-Girl is obviously *not* a gendered concept. A hiphop nightclub player is no less a Young-Girl than a *beurette** tarted up like a porn-star. The resplendent corporate advertising retiree who divides his time between the Côte d'Azur and his Paris office, where he still likes to keep an eye on things, is no less a Young-Girl than the urban single woman too obsessed with her consulting career to notice she's lost fifteen years of her life to it. And how could we account, if the Young-Girl were a gendered concept, for the secret relationship

---

* Slang for a French woman of North African descent.

between ultratrendy musclebound Marais homos and the Americanized petit-bourgeoisie happily settled in the suburbs with their plastic families?

In reality, the Young-Girl is simply the *model citizen* as redefined by consumer society since World War I, in *explicit* response to the revolutionary menace. As such, the Young-Girl is a *polar figure*, orienting, rather than dominating, outcomes.

At the beginning of the 1920s, capitalism realized that it could no longer maintain itself as the exploitation of human labor if it did not also colonize everything that is *beyond* the strict sphere of production. Faced with the challenge from socialism, capital too would have to socialize. It had to create its own culture, its own leisure, medicine, urbanism, sentimental education and its own mores, as well as a disposition toward their perpetual renewal. This was the Fordist compromise, the Welfare-State, family planning: social-democratic capitalism. For a somewhat limited submission to labor, since workers still distinguished themselves from their work, we have today substituted integration through subjective and existential conformity, that is, fundamentally, through consumption.

The formal domination of Capital has become more and more *real*. Consumer society now seeks out its best supporters from among the marginalized elements of traditional society—women and youth first, followed by homosexuals and immigrants.

To those who were minorities yesterday, and who had therefore been the most foreign, the most spontaneously *hostile* to consumer society, not having yet been bent to the dominant norms of integration, the latter ends up looking like emancipation. "Young people and their mothers," recognized Stuart Ewen, "had been the social principles of the consumer ethic." Young people, because adolescence is the "period of time with none but a consumptive relation to civil society" (Stuart Ewen, *Captains of Consciousness*). Women, because it is the sphere of *reproduction*, over which they still reign, that must be colonized. Hypostasized Youth and Femininity, abstracted and recoded into *Youthitude* and *Femininitude*, find themselves raised to the rank of ideal regulators of the integration of the Imperial citizenry. The figure of the Young-Girl combines these two determinations into one immediate, spontaneous, and perfectly desirable whole.

The tomboy comes to impose herself as a modernity more stunning than all the stars and starlets that so rapidly invaded the globalized imaginary. Albertine, encountered on the seawall of a resort town, arrives to infuse her casual and pansexual vitality into the crumbling universe of Marcel Proust's *In Search of Lost Time*. The schoolgirl lays down the law in Witold Gombrowicz's *Ferdydurke*. A new figure of authority is born and *she outclasses them all.*

IV

At the present hour, humanity, reformatted by the Spectacle and biopolitically neutralized, still thinks it's fooling someone by calling itself "citizen." Women's magazines breathe new life into a nearly-hundred-year-old wrong by finally offering their equivalent to males. All the old figures of patriarchal authority, from statesmen to bosses and cops, have become Young-Girlified, every last one of them, even the Pope.

Among its many signs, we recognize that the new physiognomy of Capital, only an inkling in the interwar years, has now attained perfection. "Once its fictive character is generalized, the 'anthropomorphosis' of Capital becomes a fait-accompli. Then the mysterious spell is revealed, thanks to which the generalized credit that rules every exchange (from banknotes to mortgage payments, from labor or marriage contracts to 'human' and familial relations, from education and the diplomas and careers that follow, to the promises of all ideologies: all exchanges are now exchanges of dilatory appearance) strikes with the image of its uniform emptiness the 'heart of darkness' of every 'personality' and every 'character.' This is how Capital's people increase, just when every ancestral distinction seems to be disappearing and every specificity of class or ethnicity. It's a fact that doesn't cease to amaze that the naïve, who still 'think' with their gaze lost in the past" (Giorgio Cesarano, *Chronicle of a Masked Ball*). The Young-Girl appears as the culminating point of this *anthropomorphosis of Capital*. The process of valorization, in the imperial phase, is no longer simply capitalist: IT COINCIDES WITH THE SOCIAL. Integration into this process, which is no longer distinct from integration into imperial "society" and which no longer rests on any "objective" base, requires that every person *permanently self-valorize*.

Society's final moment of socialization, Empire, is thus also the moment when each person is called upon to relate to themselves *as value*, that is, according to the central mediation of a series of controlled abstractions. The Young-Girl would thus be the being that no longer has any intimacy with herself *except as value*, and whose every activity, in every detail, is directed to self-valorization. At each moment, she affirms herself as the *sovereign subject* of her own reification. The unquestionable character of her power, all of the crushing assurance of this flattened being, woven exclusively by the conventions, codes, and representations fleetingly in effect, all the authority that the least of her gestures incarnates, all of this is immediately indexed to her *absolute transparency* to "society."

Precisely because of her nothingness, each of her judgments carries the imperative weight of the entire social order, *and she knows it*.

V

The theory of the Young-Girl does not simply emerge fortuitously when the genesis of the imperial order is complete and begins to be apprehended as such. That which emerges is nearing its end. And in its turn the Young-Girl party will have to break up.

As the Young-Girlist formatting becomes more widespread, competition hardens and the satisfaction linked to conformity wanes. A qualitative jump becomes necessary; it becomes urgent to equip oneself with new and unheard-of attributes: One must move into some still-virgin space. Hollywood sorrow, the political consciousness of TV news, vague neo-Buddhist spirituality, or an engagement in some consciousness-soothing collective enterprise should do the trick. Thus is born, bit by bit, *the organic Young-Girl*. The struggle for the survival of Young-Girls is from then on identified with the necessity to overcome the industrial Young-Girl, with the necessity to move on to the organic Young-Girl. Contrary to her predecessor, the organic Young-Girl no longer displays the urge for some kind of emancipation, but rather *a high-security obsession with conservation*. For Empire has been undermined at its foundations and must defend itself against entropy. Having attained the fullness of its hegemony, it can now only collapse. The organic Young-Girl would thus become responsible, ecological, "in solidarity," maternal, reasonable, "natural," respectful, more self-controlled than falsely liberated, in a word, fiendishly biopolitical. She would no longer mimic excess, but rather, moderation in all things.

As we see, when the evidence of the Young-Girl attains the force of cliché, the Young-Girl is already out of date, at least in her primitive aspect of obscenely sophisticated mass production. It is at this critical moment of transition that we enter the fray.

VI

So as not to give a false impression—which could well be our intention—the jumble of fragments that follows does not in any way constitute a theory. These are materials accumulated by chance encounter, by frequenting and observing Young-Girls: pearls extracted from magazines, expressions gleaned out of order under sometimes dubious circumstances. They are assembled here under approximate rubrics, just as they were published in *TIQQUN* 1; there was no doubt they needed a little organization. The choice to expose these elements in all their incompleteness, in their contingent original state, in their ordinary excess, knowing that if polished, hollowed out, and given a good trim they might together constitute an altogether presentable doctrine, we have chosen—just this once—*trash theory*. The cardinal ruse of theoreticians resides, generally, in the presentation of the result of their deliberations *such that the process of deliberation is no longer apparent*. We figure that, faced with Bloomesque fragmentation of attention, this ruse no longer works. We have chosen a different one. In these scattered fragments, spirits attracted to moral comfort or vice in need of condemning will find only roads leading nowhere. It is less a question of converting Young-Girls than of mapping out the dark corners of the fractalized frontline of Young-Girlization. And it is a question of furnishing arms for a struggle, step-by-step, blow-by-blow, wherever you may find yourself.

1

THE YOUNG-GIRL AS PHENOMENON

The Young-Girl is old insofar as she is *known* to be young. There is therefore no question for her of *benefiting* from this reprieve, which is to say of committing the few reasonable excesses, of experiencing the few "adventures" *expected* of people her age, and all this with an eye to the moment when she will have to settle down into the ultimate void of adulthood. Thus, during the time it takes for youth to decay, social law contains its own violations, which are in the end just exemptions.

The Young-Girl is obsessed with authenticity *because it's a lie.*

The masculine Young-Girl is paradoxical in that she's the product of a sort of "alienation by contagion." Although the feminine Young-Girl appears as the incarnation of a certain alienated masculine imaginary, there is nothing imaginary about the alienation of this incarnation. It is altogether concretely that she has eluded those whose fantasies she populates in order to face and dominate them. As the Young-Girl emancipates herself, blossoms, and multiplies, the dream turns into an all-consuming nightmare. It's at this point that her former slave returns to tyrannize yesterday's master. In the end, we witness an ironic epilogue in which the "male sex" becomes both the victim and the object of its own alienated desire.

"I want people to be beautiful."

The Young-Girl is the figure of the total and sovereign consumer; she carries herself as such in every domain of existence.

The Young-Girl knows so very well *the value of things*.

Often, before her decay has become too obvious, the Young-Girl gets married.
The Young-Girl is only good for consuming, pleasure or work, it doesn't matter.

The intimacy of the Young-Girl, now equivalent to all intimacy, has become something anonymous and exterior, an object.

The Young-Girl never creates anything; All in all, she only recreates herself.

By investing young people and women with an absurd symbolic surplus value, by making them the exclusive carriers of the two new kinds of esoteric knowledge proper to the new social order—consumption and seduction—Spectacle has effectively emancipated the slaves of the past, but it has emancipated them AS SLAVES.

> The most extreme banality of the Young-Girl is to take her/himself for an original.

The stunted quality of the Young-Girl's language, although it implies an incontestable narrowing of the field of experience, in no way constitutes a practical handicap, because it was not made to talk with, but rather to please and to repeat.

Chatter, curiosity, equivocation, hearsay, the Young-Girl incarnates the fullness of improper existence, whose categories Heidegger identified.

The Young-Girl is a lie whose apogee is the face.

When Spectacle's proclaims that woman is the future of man, it is naturally speaking of the Young-Girl, and the future it predicts recalls only the worst cybernetic slavery.

"No kidding!"

The Young-Girl manages to live with a dozen unarticulated concepts, as her only philosophy, that immediately become moral categories, meaning that the whole of her vocabulary can be definitively reduced to the Good/Evil binary. It goes without saying that, in order to consider the world, it must be sufficiently simplified, and in order to permit her to live in it happily, the world must make many martyrs, starting with herself.

"Highly visible physical imperfections, even if they have no effect on aptitude for work, weaken people socially, transforming them into the involuntary invalids of work."
(Dr. Julius Moses, *Afa-Bundeszeitung*, Februrary 1929)

In the Young-Girl, what is sweetest is also the cruelest, what is most "natural" is most feigned, what is most "human" is most machine-like.

Adolescence is a recent category created according to the demands of mass consumption.

The Young-Girl invariably calls "happiness" everything to which THEY chain her.

The Young-Girl is never simply sad, she is also sad that she's sad.

Ultimately, the Young-Girl's ideal is *domestic*.

Bloom is the crisis of classic sexuation and the Young-Girl is the offensive by which market domination has responded to this crisis.

There is no more chastity in the Young-Girl than there is debauchery. The Young-Girl simply lives as a stranger to her desires, whose coherence is governed by her market-driven superego. The ennui of abstraction flows into this come.

There is nothing, neither poetry nor ethnology, neither Marxism nor metaphysics, that the Young-Girl cannot fit into the closed horizon of her vapid quotidian.

"Albertine comes from nowhere, and is very modern in that way: she flutters, comes and goes, from her absence of attachments she derives the instability and the unpredictable quality which give her her power of freedom" (Jacques Dubois, *For Albertine: Proust and the Sense of the Social*).

When it addresses itself distinctly to the Young-Girl, the Spectacle is not above a bit of *bathmology*. This is why the entire significance of boy-bands and girl-bands comes from making a show of the very fact of making a show. The lie consists, here—by means of crude irony—in presenting as a lie what is on the contrary *the truth of the Young-Girl*.

The Young-Girl is struck by sudden vertigo whenever the world stops revolving around her.

The Young-Girl sees herself as the holder of a *sacred* power: the power of commodities.

"I love children. They're beautiful, honest, and they smell good."

The mother and the whore, as Weininger understands them, are equally present in the Young-Girl. But the one hardly renders her any more worthy of praise than the other makes her worthy of blame. In fact, over time, a curious reversibility between the two can be observed.

The Young-Girl is fascinating in the manner of all things that exhibit a closing-in-on-themselves, a mechanical self-sufficiency or an indifference to the observer, like the insect, the infant, the automaton, or Foucault's pendulum.

Why must the Young-Girl always feign some activity or other? To remain **unassailable** in her passivity.

The "freedom" of the Young-Girl rarely goes beyond the ostentatious cult of the most pathetic of the Spectacle's productions. Essentially, it consists in opposing a lack of zeal with the necessities of alienation.

THE FUTURE OF THE YOUNG-GIRL: THE NAME OF A GROUP OF "COMMUNIST" GIRLS, ORGANIZED IN THE SOUTHERN SUBURBS OF PARIS IN 1936 FOR THE *"ENTERTAINMENT, EDUCATION, AND THE DEFENSE OF THEIR INTERESTS."*

The Young-Girl wants to be desired without love or loved without desire. There is no threat, in either case, to her unhappiness.

The Young-Girl has love STORIES.

It is enough to recall what she classifies as "adventure" to get a good idea of just how much the Young-Girl fears the possible.

The old age of the Young-Girl is no less hideous than her youth. From one end to the other, her life is nothing but a progressive shipwreck in formlessness, and never an irruption of becoming. *The Young-Girl wallows in the limbo of time.*

As for the face of the Young-Girl, differences in age, like difference in gender, are insignificant. There is no age to be *struck by youthitude*, nor is there a gender that forbids itself a dash of femininitude.

> Just like the magazines THEY intend for her and which she devours so painfully, the life of the Young-Girl is divided and organized into so many columns, between which the greatest separation reigns.

THE YOUNG-GIRL IS THAT WHICH, BEING ONLY THIS, SCRUPULOUSLY OBEYS THE AUTHORITARIAN DISTRIBUTION OF ROLES.

Love for the Young-Girl is just autism for two.

What THEY continue to call virility is nothing more than the infantilism of men and femininity the infantilism of women. Moreover, perhaps one ought to speak of virilism and of "feminism" when so much voluntarism is mixed into the acquisition of an identity.

The same disabused stubbornness that characterized the traditional woman, assigned to the home with the duty of ensuring survival, blossoms, at present, in the Young-Girl, now emancipated from the domestic sphere and from all sexual monopoly. She will from now on express herself everywhere: in her irreproachable affective impermeability at work, in the extreme rationalization she imposes on her "emotional life," in her every step, so spontaneously military, in the way she fucks, carries herself, or taps away on her computer—which is no different from the way she washes her car.

"One piece of information that I obtain in a well-known Berlin department store is particularly instructive: 'When taking on sales and office staff,' says an influential gentleman from the personnel department, 'we attach most importance to a pleasant appearance.' From a distance he looks a bit like Reinhold Schunzel in early films. I ask him what he understands by 'pleasant'—saucy or pretty. 'Not exactly pretty. What's far more crucial is . . . oh, you know, a morally pink complexion.'

I do know. A morally pink complexion—this combination of concepts at a stroke renders transparent the everyday life that is fleshed out by window displays, salary-earners, and illustrated papers. Its morality must have a pink hue, its pink a moral grounding. That is what the people responsible for selection want. They would like to cover life with a varnish concealing its far-from-rosy reality. But beware, if morality should penetrate beneath the skin, and the pink be not quite moral enough to prevent the eruption of desires! The gloom of unadorned morality would bring as much danger to the prevailing order as a pink that began to flare up immorally. So that both may be neutralized, they are tied to one another. The same system that requires the aptitude test also produces this nice, friendly mixture; and the more rationalization progresses, the more the morally pink appearance gains ground. It is scarcely too hazardous to assert that in Berlin a salaried type is developing, standardized in the direction of the desired complexion. Speech, clothes, gestures, and countenances become assimilated and the result of the process is that very same pleasant appearance, which with the help of photographs can be widely reproduced. A selective breeding that is carried out under the pressure of social relations, and that is necessarily supported by the economy through the arousal of corresponding consumer needs.

Employees must join in, whether they want to or not. The rush to the numerous beauty salons springs partly from existential concerns, and the use of cosmetic products is not always a luxury. For fear of being withdrawn from use as obsolete, ladies and gentlemen dye their hair, while forty-year-olds take up sports to keep slim. 'How Can I Become Beautiful?' runs the title of a booklet recently launched on to the market; the newspaper advertisements for it say that it shows ways 'to look young and beautiful both now and forever.' Fashion and economy work hand in hand. Most people, of course, are in no position to consult a specialist. They fall prey to quacks or have to make do with remedies as cheap as they are dubious. For some time now the above-mentioned deputy Dr. Moses has been fighting in their interest in parliament, for incorporating proper provision for disfigurement into social security. The young Working Community of Cosmetic Practitioners of Germany has associated itself with this legitimate demand" (Siegfried Kracauer, *The Salaried Masses: Duty and Distraction in Weimar Germany*, 1930).

The loss of metaphysical direction is not distinct, in the Young-Girl, from the "loss of the sensory" (Arnold Gehlen) in which the extreme modernity of her alienation is verified.

The Young-Girl moves in the oblivion of Being, no less than in that of the event.

The incompressible agitation of the Young-Girl, in the image of this society at its every point, is governed by the hidden demand to render effective a false and pathetic metaphysics, whose most immediate substance is the negation of the passage of time, and the obscuring of human finitude.

THE YOUNG-GIRL RESEMBLES HER PHOTO.

Insofar as her appearance entirely exhausts her essence, as her representation does her reality, the Young-Girl is that which is entirely expressible, perfectly predictable, and absolutely neutralized.

The Young-Girl exists only in proportion to the desire that THEY have for her, and knows herself only by what THEY say she is.

The Young-Girl appears as the product and the principal outcome of the formidable surplus crisis of capitalist modernity. She is the proof and the support of the limitless pursuit of the process of valorization when the process of accumulation proves limited (by the limits of the planet itself, ecological catastrophe, or social implosion).

The Young-Girl is content to cover over with a falsely provocative hidden sense the actual *economic* sense of her motivations.

All the freedom of movement the Young-Girl enjoys in no way prevents her from being a *prisoner*, from manifesting, in every circumstance, the automatisms of the shut-in.

The way to be the Young-Girl is to be *nothing*.

Managing to "succeed in her sentimental and professional life at the same time": certain Young-Girls proclaim this as an ambition worthy of respect.

The "love" of the Young-Girl is just a word in the dictionary.

**The Young-Girl requires not only
that you protect her,
she also wants the power to educate you.**

> The eternal return of the same styles in fashion is enough to convince: The Young-Girl does not play with appearances. It is appearances that play with her.

Even more than the feminine Young-Girl, the masculine Young-Girl, with his fake muscles, absurdity, which is to say, *suffering*, in what Foucault called "the discipline of bodies": *"Discipline increases the forces of the body (in economic terms of utility) and diminishes these same forces (in political terms of obedience). In short, it dissociates power from the body; on the one hand, it turns it into an 'aptitude,' a 'capacity,' which it seeks to increase; on the other hand, it reverses the course of the energy, the power that might result from it, and turns it into a relation of strict subjection"* (*Michel Foucault*, Discipline and Punish).

"Oh, a girl, that receptacle of shame under beauty's lock and key!"
(Witold Gombrowicz, *Ferdydurke*, 1937)

**There is surely no place where one feels
as horribly alone
as in the arms of a Young-Girl.**

When the Young-Girl gives in to her own insignificance, she still manages to find glory in it, because she is "having fun."

"This was precisely what captivated me—the maturity and autonomy of her youth, the self-assurance of her style. While we, in school, had our blackheads, constantly broke out in pimples and ideals, while our movements were gawky and each step was a gaffe, her *exterior* was entrancingly polished. Youth, for her, was not a transitional age—for this modern one, youth was the only time befitting a human being. [...] Her youth had no need of ideals, it was in and of itself an ideal" (Witold Gombrowicz, *Ferdydurke*).

The Young-Girl never learns anything. That's not why she's here.

The Young-Girl knows all too well what she wants *in detail* to want anything in general.

"DON'T TOUCH MY BAG!"

The triumph of the Young-Girl originates in the failure of feminism.

The Young-Girl does not speak. On the contrary, she is *spoken* by the Spectacle.

The Young-Girl wears the mask of her face.

The Young-Girl reduces all grandeur to the level of her ass.

The Young-Girl is a purifier of negativity, an industrial profiler of unilaterality. In all things, she separates the negative from the positive, and generally retains only one of the two. No surprise that she doesn't believe in words, which in fact have no meaning in her mouth. Let it suffice, for us to be convinced, to see what she means by "romantic" which after all has little to do with Hölderlin.

"We must hence envisage the birth of the 'young girl' as the construction of an object in which different disciplines compete (from medicine to psychology, from physical education to morality, from physiology to hygiene)" (Jean-Claude Caron, *The Body of Young Girls*).

The Young-Girl would like for the simple word "love" not to imply the project of destroying this society.

"AH, THE HEART!"

"Don't confuse your job with your feelings!"
In the life of the Young-Girl, inactivated
opposites thrust into nothingness complement
each other, and never contradict.

The Young-Girl's sentimentalism and materialism,
however opposed they may appear, are really in solidarity:
two aspects of her central void.
The Young-Girl is happy to speak of her childhood
with emotion, in order to give the impression
that she has not gotten over it, that at bottom,
she is still naive. Like all whores, she dreams of
candor. But unlike whores, she insists that we
believe her, and that we believe her sincerely.
Her infantilism, which is ultimately just *a childlike
fundamentalism*, makes her the wiliest vector of
general infantilization.

The pettiest sentiments still retain, for the
Young-Girl, the prestige of their sincerity.

The Young-Girl loves her illusions
the same way she loves her reification:
by proclaiming them.

The Young-Girl knows everything as devoid
of consequences, even her own suffering.
Everything is funny, nothing's a big deal.
Everything is *cool*, nothing is serious.

The Young-Girl wants to be recognized not for what she might be, but for the simple fact of her being. She wants to be recognized in the absolute.

The Young-Girl is not here to be criticized.

When the Young-Girl arrives at the age limit of infantilism, where it becomes impossible not to ask oneself the question of ends for fear of finding oneself suddenly in search of means (which, in this society, can arrive very late), she reproduces. Paternity and maternity constitute one method among others, no less devoid of substance than all the rest, of holding out
UNDER THE EMPIRE OF NECESSITY.

THE YOUNG-GIRL DOESN'T KISS YOU,
SHE DROOLS OVER YOU THROUGH HER TEETH.
MATERIALISM OF SECRETIONS.

The Young-Girl adopts above all the point of view of psychology, about herself as much as the course of the world. This is how she manages to present a certain consciousness of her own reification, a consciousness that is itself reified, as it's cut off from all *gesture*.

The Young-Girl knows
the standard perversions.

"TOO CUTE!"

The Young-Girl's aim is *balance*. Not the balance of a ballerina, but of an accountant.

The smile has never served as an argument.
There is also the smile of **skulls**.

The Young-Girl's affectivity is made only of signs, and occasionally, mere *signals*.

Wherever *ethos* is lacking or decomposing, the Young-Girl appears as the bearer of the fleeting and discolored mores of the Spectacle.

The Young-Girl is not *expected* to understand you.

The Young-Girl's predilection for actors and actresses can be explained according to the laws of elementary magnetism: whereas they are the *positive* absence of any quality, the void that takes all forms, she is but the *negative* absence of quality. Thus, like his reflection, the actor is the same as the Young-Girl, whose negation he also is. THE YOUNG-GIRL CONCEIVES LOVE AS ONE *SPECIFIC* KIND OF ACTIVITY.

The Young-Girl's laughter rings with the desolation of nightclubs.

The Young-Girl is the only insect that consents to the *entomology of women's magazines*.

**Identical, in this, to misery,
a Young-Girl never shows up alone.**
Thus wherever Young-Girls dominate, their taste must also dominate; this is what determines the tastes of our time. The Young-Girl is the purest form of reified relations; she is their truth. The Young-Girl is the anthropological concentrate of reification.

The Spectacle amply remunerates, though indirectly, the conformity of the Young-Girl.

In love more than anywhere else, the Young-Girl behaves like an accountant, always suspecting that she loves more than she is loved, and that she gives more than she receives.

Among Young-Girls there is a community of gesture and expression that is anything but moving.

The Young-Girl is ontologically **virgin**,
virgin of all *experience*.
The Young-Girl can display solicitude, provided one is truly miserable. This is one aspect of her resentment.

The Young-Girl does not perceive the passage of time any more than she is moved by its "consequences." Otherwise, how else could she speak of aging with such indignation, as though it were a crime committed against her?

Even when she isn't trying to seduce, the Young-Girl acts like a seductress.

There is something *professional* about everything the Young-Girl does.

`The Young-Girl will never stop flattering herself for having "Common Sense."`

In the Young-Girl, even the most insipid moralisms have the air of prostitution.

The Young-Girl possesses all the severity of the economy. However, the Young-Girl is more ignorant of abandon than anything else.

The Young-Girl is the entire reality of the Spectacle's abstract codes.

The Young-Girl occupies the central node of the present system of desire.

The Young-Girl's every experience is drawn back incessantly into the preexisting representation she has made for herself. All the overwhelming concreteness, the living part of the passage of time and of things are known to her only as imperfections, as alterations of an abstract model.

The Young-Girl is resentment *that smiles.*

There are beings that give you the desire to die slowly before their eyes, but the Young-Girl only excites the desire to vanquish her, to take advantage of her.

THE YOUNG-GIRL DOES NOT COUPLE
IN TRANSPORT TOWARD THE OTHER,
BUT IN ORDER TO ESCAPE HER UNBEARABLE NULLITY.

The supposed liberation of women did not consist in their emancipation from the domestic sphere, but rather in the total extension of the domestic into all of society.

In the face of any person who would seek to make her think, the Young-Girl will always pride herself on being a realist.

Insofar as what she hides is not her secret, but rather *her shame*, the Young-Girl hates the unexpected, especially when it is not programmed.

"Being in love:
a drug that reduces stress."

The Young-Girl never stops repeating it: She wants to be loved *for who she is*, which is to say for the non-being she is.

The Young-Girl is the living and continual introjection of all repression.

The "self" of the Young-Girl is as thick as a magazine.

Nothing, in the conduct of the Young-Girl, has a reason in itself. Everything is ordered by the dominant definition of happiness. The Young-Girl's estrangement from herself borders on mythomania.

As a last resort, the Young-Girl fetishizes "love" so as to avoid an awareness of the entirely conditioned nature of her desires.

"I'm so happy I could give a shit about being free!"

"THE CHEMISTRY OF PASSION: Today, everything is explainable, even the fact of falling in love! Farewell romanticism, since the 'phenomenon' is just a series of chemical reactions."

In their divorce,
the Young-Girl's heart and ass
have become two empty abstractions.

"The ghostly image of the cinema hero model[s] the embraces of adolescents, and later adultery" (Max Horkheimer/ Theodor W. Adorno, *The Dialectic of Enlightenment*).

The Young-Girl is steeped in déjà-vu. For her, the first-time experience is always a second time in representation.

Naturally, nowhere has there been a "sexual liberation"—that oxymoron!—but only the pulverization of everything that slowed the total mobilization of desire in view of the *production* of merchandise. The "tyranny of pleasure" does not incriminate pleasure, but tyranny.

The Young-Girl knows how to take feelings into account.

In the world of Young-Girls, coitus appears as the logical sanction of all experience.

The Young-Girl is "satisfied with life," at least that's what she says.

The Young-Girl only establishes relationships based on the strictest reification and on false substantiality, where THEY can be sure that what unites in fact only separates.

The Young-Girl is optimistic, thrilled, positive, happy, enthusiastic, joyful; in other words, ***she suffers.***

The Young-Girl is produced wherever nihilism begins to speak of happiness.

There is nothing special about the Young-Girl; that is her "beauty."

The Young-Girl is an optical illusion.

From afar, she is an angel, and up close, she is a beast.

The Young-Girl doesn't age. She decomposes.

We know, in general, what the Young-Girl thinks of *worrying*.

The Young-Girl's education is the inverse of all other forms of education: First the immediate innate perfection of youth, then the effort to maintain herself at the height of this primary nullity, and finally, collapse in the face of the impossibility of returning to this side of time.

Viewed from afar, the Young-Girl's nothingness appears relatively habitable, at certain moments even comfortable.

"Love, Work, Health."

The Young-Girl's "beauty" is never a particular beauty, or one that might belong to her. On the contrary, hers is a beauty without content, an absolute beauty free of any personality. The Young-Girl's "beauty" is but the form of a void, the spectral form of the Young-Girl.

And this is why she can, without choking on her words, speak of "beauty," because her own is never the expression of a substantial singularity, but a pure and ghostly objectivity.

> "Indeed, only now does [the basic ideological confusion between woman and sexuality] assume its full scope since women, once *subjugated* as a sex, are today '*liberated*' as a sex [...] Women, young people and the body—the emergence of all of which after thousands of years of servitude and forgetting

in effect constitutes the most revolutionary potentiality—and, therefore, the most fundamental risk for any social order whatever—are integrated and recuperated as a 'myth of emancipation.' Women are given Woman to consume, the young are given the Young and, in this formal and narcissistic emancipation, their real liberation is successfully averted" (Jean-Trissotin Baudrillard, *The Consumer Society: Myths and Structures*).

The Young-Girl offers an unequivocal model of the metropolitan ethos: a refrigerated consciousness living in exile in a plasticized body.

"Too cool!!!" Instead of saying "very" the Young-Girl says "too," while in fact, she is so very little.

2

THE YOUNG-GIRL AS TECHNIQUE OF THE SELF

"What is Pleasure?"

There is nothing in the Young-Girl's life, even in the deepest zones of her intimacy, that escapes alienated reflexivity, that escapes the codification and the gaze of the Spectacle. This intimacy strewn with commodities yields entirely to advertising, and is entirely socialized *as intimacy*, which is to say that she is part-for-part subject to a fallacious commonality that does not allow her to express herself.

For the Young-Girl, what is most secret is also most public.

The Young-Girl's body is an encumbrance, it is her world and it is her prison.

The Young-Girl's physiology is the offensive glaze of her false substantiality.

The Young-Girl desires the Young-Girl.

The Young-Girl is the Young-Girl's ideal.

"Tired of macho guys? Why not try an objectified man..."

The rhetoric of the war of the sexes, and thus for now, of women's revenge, operates as the ultimate ruse through which the logic of virility will have vanquished women without their knowledge: by enclosing them, at the price of a simple role reversal, in the submission/domination alternative, to the exclusion of all else.

"What does the mortification of the body require? That we nourish a sacred and implacable hate for our bodies" (Spiritual Instructions for the Sisters of Saint Vincent-de-Paul, 1884).

The Young-Girl tries to express the self-referential closing-in-on-herself and the systematic ignorance of *lack*. This is why she is without defect, in the same way she is without perfection.

In fairly recent prehistory, when there were only women's magazines for women, a rumor lasting the length of a season suggested that these magazines had a depressing effect on their readers. Here and there one heard, based on an "American scientific study," the most meager gossip of the age, that whenever a woman closed one of them she was noticeably sadder than before she'd opened it—she produced less serotonin, no doubt. And it is true, for whoever has tried to catch a Young-Girl in the midst of such an exercise will have noted her air of concern, of anguished seriousness and haste in turning the pages, as though picking through the rosary of an unloved religion. It seems that the act of contrition, in Empire's religion of biopolitics, has managed to survive quite well, indeed, having only become more *immanent*.

"I'm gonna do whatever I want with my hair!"

The Young-Girl methodically reinvests everything from which she has been liberated with pure servitude. (It would be good, for example, to ask oneself what *contemporary woman*, which is a fairly terrible species of Young-Girl, has done with the "liberty" that the struggles of feminism have won her.)

The Young-Girl is an attribute of her own *program*, in which everything must be regimented.

"AT TWELVE YEARS OLD, I DECIDED TO BE BEAUTIFUL."

The tautological nature of the Young-Girl's beauty is rooted in the fact that she sees no alterity, but only the ideal representation of herself. This explains why her supposed interlocutor is thrown into such a terrible space, even if he is free to believe, idiotically, that she is meant for him. The Young-Girl establishes a space of *power* insofar as this space is not, in the end, *a means* to approach her.

The Young-Girl *has* sexuality in the exact proportion to which all sensuality is foreign to her.

"In consequence, the biologization of sex in particular and of the body in general establishes the body of the young girl as the ideal laboratory for the medical gaze" (Jean-Claude Caron, *The Body of Young Girls*).

The "youth" and "femininity" of the Young-Girl, in fact her youthitude and femininitude, are that through which the control of appearances extends to the discipline of bodies.

The Young-Girl considers her ass a sufficient foundation for her sentiment of incommunicable singularity.

The Young-Girl is so psychological... She has succeeded in rendering herself as *flat* as the object of psychology.

It is in the very being of the Young-Girl to reduce the metaphysical fact of finitude to a simple question of *technique*: which is the most effective anti-wrinkle cream? The most moving characteristic of the Young-

Girl is doubtless this maniacal effort of attaining, in her appearance, a definitive impermeability to time and space, to history and her environment, to be everywhere and always *impeccable*.

Protestant ethics, rejected as a general principal of how society functions and as a behavioral norm since the end of the "morality of producers," has at the same time, and more rapidly since World War II, been wholly taken up at the level of the individual: since then it has massively governed the relation people have with their own bodies, their passions, and their lives, all of which they economize.

Certainly because eroticism presents itself to the Young-Girl in all the unquestionable positivity that is inevitably attached to sexuality, and because transgression itself has become a tranquil norm, isolatable and encoded, coitus is not among those things that, in the relations one entertains with the Young-Girl, allows you to advance beyond a certain exteriority; rather, it locks you in this exteriority.

"NEW BREASTS FOR MY 18TH BIRTHDAY."

The "youth" that the Spectacle has granted the Young-Girl is a very bitter gift, for this "youth" is what is incessantly LOST.

What is living need not express itself too much. What is dying dissipates in rattle the obvious approach of its end. The Young-Girl's excessive affirmation of her sexuation attests to the agony of classical sexuation, that is, to *its material basis*. The spectre of Man and Woman haunts the streets of the metropolis. Its muscles come from the gym, her breasts are silicone.

Between the Young-Girl and the world there is a *window*. Nothing touches the Young-Girl, the Young-Girl touches nothing.

Nothing in the identity of the Young-Girl truly belongs to her, even less her "youth" than her "femininity." She does not possess attributes, instead, her attributes possess her, those THEY have so generously loaned her.

The Young-Girl chases after health

as though it were salvation.

The sense of the self as meat, as the heap of an organ variously filled with ovaries or flanked by balls, is the basis from which emerge the aspiration and finally the failure of the Young-Girl to give herself form, or at the very least to simulate one. This feeling is not merely a lived consequence of the aberrations of Western metaphysics—which wants the formless to precede form, brought to it *from outside*—it is also what market domination must perpetuate at all cost, and which it constantly produces by rendering all bodies equivalent, by degenerating forms-of-life, by continually imposing an undifferentiating confusion. The loss of contact with the self, the crushing of all intimacy with the self, which makes the sense of self meat—these form the condition *sine qua non* for readopting the techniques of the self that the Empire offers for consumption.

The depth of penetration of this consumer junk can be read in the intensity of the feeling of the self as meat.

The exhausting
ownership of bodies

The feeling of contradiction between one's existence as a social being and one's existence as a singular being, which tears Bloom apart, does not enter the Young-Girl, who doesn't have a singular existence anymore than she has feelings in general.

"ME & MY BREASTS, MY BELLY BUTTON, MY BUTT, MY LEGS: A JOURNAL OF MY BODY"

The Young-Girl is her own jailer, prisoner in a body-made-sign inside of a language made of bodies.

"Oh this cult, this obedience, the girl's slavery just because she is a schoolgirl and because she's modern! [...] Oh, this was slavery to the point of self-effacement for the sake of style, what obedience on the girl's part!" (Gombrowicz, *Ferdydurke*).

"The profoundly-rooted instinct in women, which pushes them to use perfumes, is the manifestation of a law of biology. *The first duty of a woman is to be attractive...* Your degree of intelligence or independence is of little importance, if you do not manage to influence the men you encounter, whether consciously or not, you are not fulfilling your fundamental duty as a woman..." (Advertisement for a perfume from the 1920s in the United States).

The Young-Girl conceives her own existence as a ***management*** problem that it is her job to resolve.

Before designating a relation to the other, a social relation or a form of symbolic integration, the Young-Girl designates a relation to the self, which is to say, *to time.*

Contrary to all appearances, the Young-Girl is not worried about herself. She is not, strictly speaking, egotistical, nor for that matter egocentric, which is why her "self" is also another. That to which she consecrates all of the care of intransigent piety is for her, in fact, an exterior reality: her "body."

> The application of capital-form to all things—health capital, sun capital, sympathy capital, etc.—and more particularly to bodies, means that the alienated social totality now mediates relations once ruled by immediacy.

In the Young-Girl, the tension between convention and nature apparently disappears as the meaning of the terms is lost, so much so that one never seems to do violence to the other.

The Young-Girl is like capitalism, domestic servants, and protozoa: She knows how to adapt and what's more, she's proud of it.

Contrary to what is true of traditional societies, which recognized the existence of abject things and exposed them *as such*, the Young-Girl denies their existence and dissimulates them.

The appearance of the Young-Girl is the Young-Girl herself. Between the two there is nothing.

Like all slaves, the Young-Girl thinks that she is the object of much more surveillance than she really is.

The Young-Girl's absence to herself is not contradicted by any of the "care" she seems to show for herself.

The Young-Girl is never plastic
enough for her taste.

The Young-Girl doesn't like wrinkles,
wrinkles do not conform;
wrinkles are the writing of life;
life does not conform.
The Young-Girl is as terrified of wrinkles as she is
of all true EXPRESSION.

In the guise of self-consciousness, the Young-Girl only has a vague sense of life.

For the Young-Girl, bare life
still functions as clothing.

The Young-Girl lives sequestered inside her own "beauty."

The Young-Girl doesn't love, she loves herself loving.

"Zen, Speed, Organic: 3 lifestyle diets."

The Young-Girl does not go as far as requiring that the short-lived conventions to which she submits have any *meaning*.

The Young-Girl understands all relations on the model of the *contract*, more precisely, a contract that can be *revoked* at any point according to the interests of the signatories. It is a form of bargaining about the differential value of each actor in the seduction market, in which it is necessary, in the end, for someone to pocket the dividends.

"Are you OK with your body?
Is your young carcass, dressed in graceful curves, well-maintained? Is your frame solid? The linings silky? Are you in good shape?"

The Young-Girl produces herself *daily* as such, via the maniacal reproduction of the dominant *ethos*.

"How to lose ten years with the right lifestyle."

A cosmetics multinational recently launched a major advertising campaign for an anti-wrinkle cream by the name of *Ethic*. In so doing, it simultaneously revealed that there is nothing as *ethical* as covering oneself in shit every morning in order to conform to the categorical imperative of youthitude, and that there could not possibly be any *ethos* other than that of the Young-Girl.

"Beauty" is the mode of unveiling proper to the Young-Girl in the Spectacle. This is why she is also a *generic product,* containing all of the abstraction of that which is forced to address itself to a certain segment of the sexual market-place, inside of which *everything looks alike.*

Capitalism has truly created wealth, because it *discovered* it where it had formerly been invisible. This is how, for example, capitalism created beauty, health, or youth *as wealth,* that is, as qualities that possess you.

The Young-Girl is never satisfied with her submission to consumer metaphysics, with the docility of her entire being, and obviously of her entire body, to the norms of the Spectacle. This is why she displays the need to exhibit it.

"They have offended the thing I hold most dear: my image" (Silvio Berlusconi).

The Young-Girl always-already lives as a couple, that is, she lives with her image.

The Young-Girl confirms the psychological import of consumer semiocracy.

"HOW MUCH BEAUTY HAVE YOU GOT? NO, BEAUTY IS NOT A QUESTION OF SUBJECTIVE APPRECIATION. UNLIKE CHARM, MUCH TOO FLUID A NOTION, BEAUTY IS CALCULATED IN CENTIMETERS, DIVIDED

INTO FRACTIONS, WEIGHED, EXAMINED BY MAGNI-
FYING GLASS, EVALUATED IN ITS THOUSANDS OF SLY
DETAILS. STOP HIDING BEHIND NEO-HIPPY PRINCI-
PLES, LIKE 'INNER BEAUTY, THAT'S WHAT COUNTS,'
'I'VE GOT MY OWN STYLE,' AND DARE TO MEASURE
YOURSELVES IN THE COURT OF THE GREATS!!!"

The Young-Girl's beauty is *produced*. She doesn't
mind saying so: "Beauty doesn't fall from the sky,"
that is, it's the fruit of labor.

The Young-Girl's self-control and self-constraint
are obtained through the introjection of two
unquestionable "necessities": that of *reputation*
and that of *health*.

*"Today, not suffering is not a luxury.
It's a right."*

**Officially, the Young-Girl has preferred
to become a thing that feels,
rather than a Bloom who suffers.**
The Young-Girl pursues plastic perfection in all its
forms, in particular, her own.

From **working out** to anti-wrinkle creams
and liposuction, the Young-Girl's determination
is the same regardless—to disregard her body, and
to make her body an abstraction.

"Anything you can do to come to terms with your image."

However vast her narcissism, the Young-Girl doesn't love herself; what she loves is "her" *image*, that is, something that is not only foreign and exterior to her, but that *possesses* her, in the full sense of the word. The Young-Girl lives under the tyranny of this ungrateful master.

AS A LAST RESORT, THE YOUNG-GIRL DRAPES HERSELF IN HER OWN LACK OF MYSTERY.

THE YOUNG-GIRL IS FIRST AND FOREMOST A POINT OF VIEW ON THE PASSAGE OF TIME.

BUT A POINT OF VIEW THAT IS ALIVE.

3

THE YOUNG-GIRL AS SOCIAL RELATION

**The Young-Girl is the elementary social relation,
the central form of the desire of desire in the Spectacle.**

And meanwhile, love has been lost in the
most foulest of spectacular role-plays.

The Young-Girl never gives herself; she only gives
what she has, which is to say the array of qualities that
THEY loan her. This is also why it is not possible to
love the Young-Girl, but only to consume her.

"I CAN'T GET ATTACHED, OK?"

Seduction is an aspect of social labor: that of the Young-Girl.
The Young-Girl's impotence or frigidity concretely
manifest that her own erotic power is detached from
her and autonomized to the point of dominating her.

When the Young-Girl giggles, she's working.

The Young-Girl's reification fits so well into the world of the authoritarian commodity that it should be considered her fundamental professional skill.

Sexuality is every bit as central for the Young-Girl as each one of her couplings is insignificant.

And they are realistic, even in love.

The Young-Girl does not content herself with the belief that sexuality exists. She swears she has encountered it. For new gods, new superstitions.

"What's a good screw?"

Never forget that the Young-Girl who loves you also *chose* you.

"Lovesickness can make you lose seven pounds."

For the Young-Girl, seduction never ends, which is to say that the Young-Girl ends with seduction.

Every relation with the Young-Girl consists in being chosen anew at every instant. In this it imposes the same contractual precarity as work does.

The Young-Girl doesn't love anyone, which is to say that she only loves the impersonality of THEM. She manages to detect the Spectacle wherever it is to be found, and wherever she finds it, she adores it.

Because in the Spectacle, even "carnal union" opportunely increases separation.

"BELIEVE IN BEAUTY."

The "dictatorship of beauty" is also the dictatorship of ugliness. It does not signify the brutal hegemony of a certain paradigm of beauty, but rather, more radically, the hegemony of the *physical simulacrum* as the form of the objectivity of beings. Understood as such, we can see that nothing prevents such a dictatorship from extending over everyone— the beautiful, the ugly, and the indifferent.

The Young-Girl does not mind miming submission here and there: *because she knows it dominates*. Something in this brings her in line with the masochism that has long been taught to women, which makes them cede the *signs* of power to men in order to recover, internally, the certitude that they possess them in *reality*.

Sexuality does not exist.

It is an abstraction, a moment of human relations that has been detached, hypostasized, and rendered ghostly.

The Young-Girl only feels at home in relationships of pure exteriority.

The Young-Girl is both production and a factor of production, that is, she is the consumer, the producer, the consumer of producers, and the producer of consumers.

The Young-Girl's "femininity" designates only the fact that the Spectacle has turned the legendary intimacy of "Woman" with nature into absolute intimacy with the "second nature" of Spectacle.

"Customize your couple!"

*The couple: to petrify all of the uncontrollable fluidity of distance between bodies by carving out a territory that can be appropriated for **intimacy**.*

The Young-Girl gives the word "desire" a very particular meaning. Make no mistake: In her mouth, it does not designate the inclination that a mortal being might feel for another mortal being or for anything, but rather, on the impersonal plane of value: *a difference of potential*. It is not this being's tension towards its object, but rather a tension in the dull *electrical* sense of a motor imbalance.

Seduction is not originally the spontaneous relation between men and women, but rather the dominant relation of men *amongst themselves*. Thus seduction always had sexuality as an empty center, but a center which was repulsive even before its effect was reversed. Shame and exhibitionism are the opposing poles of an identical fiction.

Through the eyes of the Young-Girl, the Spectacle is looking at you.

The Young-Girl's existential posture has quickly irradiated every field of human activity. In architecture, it is called *façadism*, for example.

The Young-Girl possesses her reality outside of herself, in the Spectacle, in all of the doctored representations of the ideal that it traffics, in the fleeting conventions it decrees, in the mores through which it commands mimesis. She is simply the insubstantial concretion of all these abstractions, which precede and follow her. In other words, she is a purely ideological creature.

> "Cerebral control freak, frigid obsessive, dynamic performer, unstable creative type, energetic control-freak, friendly emotional type, repressed sensitive type, emotional volunteer. Who are you really?"

THE ESSENCE OF THE YOUNG-GIRL IS TAXONOMICAL.

Among the relations monads can have amongst themselves, seduction is the one that most conforms to their essence. Seduction's fundamental hypothesis is the completeness and impermeability of the two parties. An impermeability to what she nevertheless embraces—that is what the Young-Girl calls "respect."

Flirtation is the most obvious realm of the *mechanical* functioning of relationships in consumer society.

"From all this we see that fashion furnishes an ideal field for individuals with dependent natures, whose self-consciousness, however, requires a certain amount of prominence, attention, and singularity. Fashion raises even the unimportant individual by making him the representative of a class, the embodiment of a joint spirit. [...] It is peculiarly characteristic of fashion that it renders possible a social obedience, which at the same time is a form of individual differentiation. [...] it is the mingling of the sensation of rulership with submission, the influence of which is here at work" (Georg Simmel, *Fashion*).

The blackmailing of the couple is increasingly becoming the blackmailing of sexuality. But this process has doubled in turn: The Young-Girl really only allows "best friends" to get close, in whom all sexual latency has been extinguished in advance, and none will be held at a greater distance than those she has let into her bed. It is the experience of this distance that substitutes the *partner* for the lover.

The behavior of the Young-Girl betrays *her obsession for calculation.*

"If she were mine, she would never belong only to me, nor should she. Beauty is there for everyone to see: It is a public institution" (Carlo Dossi, *Amori*, 1887).

In her own way, the Young-Girl is aiming for "zero flaws." This is why she extends first to herself the regime ruling the production of things. Her imperialism is not extraneous to the intention of serving as the example for all other Blooms.

All the Young-Girl's activity, to which she has abdicated all liberty and into which she continually loses herself, is *cosmetic* in nature. In this way she resembles the whole of society, which devotes such care to the maintenance of its facade.

The Young-Girl has taken to calling the reified set of her own limitations her "personality." She can thus assert her right to nullity as a right to "be herself," that is, to be only that, a right that must be conquered and defended.

For sexuality to have spread into every sphere of human existence, it was first necessary for THEM to fantasmatically dissociate it as a moment separated from the totality of the rest of life.

The body of the Young-Girl is merely a concession THEY have made to her, more or less durably, which explains the hatred she has for it. Her body is just a rented residence, something from which she can only derive usufruct, meaning only her *use* of it is free, and moreover, because its very walls—her corporeality projected as capital, a factor of production and consumption—are possessed by the autonomized social totality.

"Who does he think he is!?"

The Young-Girl is a form of "social relation" in the primary sense of what *relates* you to this society.

"The Perfect Sexual Relationship cannot
   be improvised:
               you decide on it
                  prepare for it
                     plan it!"

The Young-Girl's love affairs are *work*
                and like all work
             they have become *precarious*.

As identities without substance, "virility" and "femininity" are but useful tools in the Spectacle's management of social relations. They are fetishes necessary to the circulation and consumption of other fetishes.

The Spectacle loves itself, desires itself, admires itself, in the Young-Girl, its Pygmalion.

Caught inside herself, the Young-Girl doesn't express anything. She is a sign whose meaning is elsewhere.

The Young-Girl is an instrument of degradation: Everything that comes into contact with her is degraded into a Young-Girl.

"Living together and every man for himself."

The Young-Girl is the extreme point of alienated socialization, at which the most socialized person is also the most asocial.

In sexuality, as with money, it is the relations that become autonomized from what they put into relation.

It is precisely by imparting to her body, but more generally to her whole being, the character of *capital* that THEY have dispossessed the Young-Girl of both body and being.

Sexuality is a separation device. In it, THEY have made socially acceptable the fiction of a sphere of truth of all relations and beings, in which the distance between self and self, as with the distance between self and other, can finally be abolished, where pure coincidence can be found. The fiction of sexuality presents the truth/appearance, sincerity/falsehood alternative in such a way that all that is not sexuality is rejected as falsehood. It preemptively undermines any possibility of *developing* relations between beings. The art of distances, through which one can experiment with leaving separation, is constructed against the device of "sexuality" and its binary extortion.

The Young-Girl is also a design element, a precarious floating wall of the "modern" conditions of existence.

Even in love, the Young-Girl speaks the language of political economy and management.

The whole world of the Spectacle is a mirror that shows the Young-Girl the assimilable image of her ideal.

In the world of the Young-Girl, the demand for liberty comes clothed in the demand for seduction.

The Young-Girl is the anecdote of the world, and the domination of the world of the anecdote.

"**Job**. You are entering a highly constructive period that is energetically driving you forward. Everything is coming together: luck, creativity, popularity.
Love. Your charm is bringing you lots of positive feedback."

For the Young-Girl, the language of horoscopes is also "the language of real life."

The Young-Girl displays the specifically magical ability to convert the most heterogeneous "qualities" (fortune, beauty, intelligence, generosity, humor, social origins, etc.) into a single "social value" governing her every relational choice.

The Spectacle seeks to awaken the Young-Girl sleeping in everyone. This is the uniformity whose phantasm it pursues.

> The deception of porn is that it claims to represent the obscene, making visible the point at which all representation evaporates. In reality, any family meal, any managerial meeting is more obscene than a facial ejaculation.

There isn't room for two in the body of the Young-Girl.

The Young-Girl's desire to convert herself into a sign simply expresses her desire to *belong* at all costs to the society of non-belonging. It signifies a *constant* effort to remain in harmony with her visible being. The challenge explains the fanaticism.

> Under modern conditions of production, to love is impossible. In the way in which a

commodity is unveiled, gift-giving appears either as an absurd weakness, or as taking place within a flux of other exchanges and thus governed by "calculated disinterest." Since man is supposed to know only his own interests, and only to the extent that these don't ever fully emerge, only falsehood and simulation are plausible. Thus, when it comes to the intentions and real motivations of the other, paranoid suspicion reigns: The gift is so suspect that it becomes necessary to *pay to give*. The Young-Girl knows this better than anyone.

The dirty game of seduction

When private property is emptied of all of its metaphysical substance, it does not immediately die. It survives, but its content is then only negative: the right to deprive others of the use of our assets. As soon as coitus is freed from any immanent meaning, it proliferates. But in the end, it is only the ephemeral monopoly on the use of the genital organs of the other.

With the Young-Girl, the superficiality of being is caused by the superficiality of all relations.

4

THE YOUNG-GIRL AS COMMODITY

The Young-Girl isn't as worried about possessing the equivalent of what she's worth on the market-place of desire as she is about assuring herself of her *value*, which she wants to know with certitude and precision, according to the thousand signs remaining for her to convert into what she'll call her "seduction potential," in other words, her *mana*.

"She who has not found a way to give herself will find a way to sell herself" (Stendhal).

"How to be sexy without coming across as a bitch."

The value of the Young-Girl is not based on some inte-rior, or simply intrinsic, ground, but solely on her exchangeability. The value of the Young-Girl only becomes apparent in her relation to another Young-

Girl. This is why she is never alone. In making the other Young-Girl her equal in value, she puts herself into relation with herself as value. In putting herself into relation with herself as value, she differentiates herself from herself as a singular being. "Representing itself as something differentiated from itself, it begins to show itself, in reality, as a commodity" (Marx).

The Young-Girl is the commodity that insists on being consumed, at every instant, because at every instant she becomes more obsolete.

The Young-Girl doesn't contain within herself that for which she is desired: her Publicity.

The Young-Girl is an absolute: She is bought because she has value, she has value because she is bought. The tautology of commodities.

The Young-Girl is the one who has preferred to *become* a commodity, rather than passively suffer its tyranny.

In love as in the rest of this "society," nobody is expected to ignore his or her own value.

The Young-Girl is the place where products and the human coexist in an *apparently* non-contradictory manner.

The world of the Young-Girl evinces a singular sophistication, in which reification has made added progress: In it, *human relations mask market relations which mask human relations*.

"You deserve better than that guy/chick."

The Young-Girl inhabits the Spectacle just like a woman in the primitive world, as an *object* of Advertising. But the Young-Girl is also the subject of Advertising, exchanging itself. This schism in the Young-Girl is her fundamental alienation. To which is added the following drama: Whereas exogamy effectively maintained permanent ties between tribes, the Young-Girl's *mana* slips through her fingers, her Advertising fails, and it is *she herself* who suffers the consequences.

The Young-Girl is lost in her price.
That's all she is now, *and she's sick to her stomach*.

> Shame for the Young-Girl doesn't come from being bought, but rather from *not being bought*. She derives glory from her value, and even more glory from putting a price on herself.

```
Nothing  is  less  personal  than  the
"personal value" of the Young-Girl.
```

It isn't rare that, through an abuse of language that slowly becomes an abuse of reality, the owners of a unique or precious object develop an affection for a thing, and finally claim to "love" it, even "to love it a lot." Likewise, some "love" a Young-Girl. Of course, if it was truly the case they would all die of sorrow. The Young-Girl sets in motion the self-commodification of what is beyond the market; the auto-estimation of the inestimable.

"uh... no, not on the first date."

The "personal value" of the Young-Girl is simply the "price" at which she is willing to be exchanged, and it is the reason why she enters exchange so rarely—in order to increase her value.

The Young-Girl sells her existence
like it's a private service.

The Young-Girl continues to count out the incalculable she gives.

In the exchange initiated by the Young-Girl, the personal is traded against the personal on the terrain of the impersonal marketplace.

The Young-Girl, by nature bothered by love, only allows herself to be approached conditionally, con-clusively, or with a sale in mind. Even when she seems to abandon herself completely, she only abandons the part of herself that is under contract, preserving or reserving the liberty she hasn't alienated.

Because the contract can never subjugate the *entirety* of the person selling herself, some portion of her must always remain outside the contract, precisely to contract with others. The abject character of love in its current incarnation cannot be explained more clearly or with greater verisimilitude. "From this one could conclude that the absoluteness of the relationship has been perverted from the onset and that, in a mercantile society, there is indeed commerce between beings but never a veritable 'community,' never a knowledge that is more than an exchange of 'good' procedures, be they as extreme as is conceivable. Power relationships in which it is the one who pays or supports who is dominated, frustrated by his very power which measures only his 'impotence'" (Maurice Blanchot, *The Unavowable Community*).

"Hold on tight!"

The Young-Girl remains at all times the staunch owner of her body.

> She is a waitress, model, publicist, or promoter. Today, the Young-Girl sells her "power of seduction" the way her "labor power" used to be sold.

Every success in seduction is essentially a failure, for, just as we do not buy a commodity, but rather a commodity that *wants* to be bought, it is not a Young-Girl we seduce, but rather a Young-Girl who *wants* to be seduced.

The broker of a fairly singular brand of transaction, the Young-Girl trains all her efforts toward *achieving a good fuck.*

The diversity of social, geographic, or morphological constraints weighing on each grouping of human organs that the Young-Girl encounters are not sufficient to explain her differential positioning among competing products. Their exchange value is neither based on any singular expression nor on any substantial determination that could truly be made equivalent, not even through the powerful mediation of the Spectacle. This value is therefore not determined by some imaginary natural factors, but rather by the sum of *labor* furnished by each individual in order to render himself *recognizable* in the vitreous eyes of the Spectacle, that is, in order to produce himself as the *sign* of the qualities recognized by alienated Advertising, and which are never, finally, but synonyms for submission.

The Young-Girl's primary skill:
arranging for her own scarcity.

Relaxing, for the Young-Girl, consists in knowing *exactly* what she's *worth.*

"What an insult! Rejected by an old guy!"

The Young-Girl is never worried about herself, but only about her *value*. Thus, when she encounters hatred, she is struck by doubt: Has her market value dropped?

If it were worth it to them to speak, Young-Girls would say: "Our use-value may interest men, but it does not belong to us as objects. What does belong to us as objects, however, is our value. Our own intercourse as commodities proves it. We relate to each other merely as exchange-values" (Karl Marx, *Capital*).

"Seduce usefully.
Don't waste your time attracting just anybody."

The Young-Girl relates to herself in the same way that she relates to all of the products with which she surrounds herself.

"Don't devalue yourself like that!"

For the Young-Girl, it is first and foremost a matter of *making herself worth something*.

Just as an object acquired by a certain sum of money becomes pathetic compared to the infinite virtualities that this sum contained, the sexual object that the Young-Girl possesses is but a deceptive crystallization of her "seduction potential." Actual sex is but the poor objectification of all the coitus that she could just as well engage in. The Young-Girl's derision of all things is the mark of a religious intuition that has fallen into the wrong infinitude.

The Young-Girl is the most authoritarian commodity in the world of authoritarian commodities, the one that nobody can fully possess and that nevertheless polices you and can be withdrawn from you at any moment.

The Young-Girl is the commodity that claims to single out its acquirer sovereignly.

The Young-Girl lives
at home
among commodities,
which are her sisters.

The absolute triumph of the Young-Girl reveals that sociality shall henceforth be the most precious, most prized commodity of all.

What characterizes the imperial period, that of the Spectacle and Biopower, is that the Young-Girl's own body takes on the form of a commodity that belongs to her. "On the other hand, it is only at this moment that the commodity form of human beings becomes generalized" (Karl Marx).

The vitrified aspect of the face of the Young-Girl must be explained by her status as commodity: She is the *crystallization* of a certain quantity of *labor* spent to put her in accordance with the norms of a certain type of exchange. And the form of the Young-Girl's appearance, which is also that of a commodity, is characterized by the obscuring, if not the voluntary forgetting, of this concrete labor.

In the Young-Girl's "love life," a relationship between things takes the phantasmagorical form of a relationship between singular beings.

With the Young-Girl, it is not only that commodities take hold of human subjectivity. It is human subjectivity that first reveals itself as the interiorization of commodities.

One has to think that Marx didn't have the Young-Girl in mind when he wrote that "commodities cannot go to market and make exchanges of their own account."

"Originality" is part of the Young-Girl's system of banality. It is this concept that allows her to make all singularities equivalent as pure, empty singularities. In her eyes, all nonconformity takes place in a kind of nonconformist conformity.

"My boyfriend's a poet."

It is always surprising to see how the theory of comparative advantage, developed by Ricardo, is more fully verified in the commerce of Young-Girls than in that of inert goods.

It is only in exchange that the Young-Girl *attains* her value.

From the provinces, from the suburbs, or from rich neighborhoods, insofar as they're Young-Girls, all Young-Girls are equivalent.

A commodity is the materialization of a relation, the Young-Girl is its *incarnation*.

In our time, the Young-Girl is the commodity most in demand: *the human commodity*.

Within the mode of unveiling of the commodity, in which "beauty" unveils nothing of its own, appearance having become autonomous of all essence, the Young-Girl, no matter what she does, cannot escape giving herself to just *anyone*.

"Whatever, if not her then somebody else…"

The "laws of the market" have been *individualized* in the Young-Girl.

What THEY still call "love" is nothing but fetishism attached to a particular commodity: the human commodity.

The eye of the Young-Girl carries within it the effective entering-into-equivalence of all places, all things, and all beings. Thus the Young-Girl can consciously reduce everything that enters her field of perception to something she already knows from alienated Advertising. This is what her language is continually translating, full as it is of "like"… "kinda"… and other "stuff"…

The Young-Girl is a central aspect of what Negrists call "the putting-to-work of desire and affect," forever dazzled as they are by this world of commodities in which they still find nothing worthy of reproach.

> **"Seduction: learn love marketing!**
> You dream about him, he doesn't notice. Snag him with the laws of marketing. No man can resist a well-conceived marketing campaign. Especially if the product is you."

WHERE THE SPECTACLE REIGNS, THE VALUE OF THE YOUNG-GIRL IS IMMEDIATELY EFFECTIVE: HER BEAUTY ITSELF IS FELT AS *EXECUTIVE POWER*.

In order to conserve her "scarcity value," the Young-Girl must sell herself only at the highest price, which signifies that she must usually give up selling herself. Thus, as we often see, the Young-Girl is an opportunist even in abstinence.

"...Because I'm worth it!"

In classical economic terms, we have to admit that the Young-Girl is a "Giffen good" or "Giffenian," that is, an object, as opposed to what "usually" takes place, whose demand rises the more expensive it is. This category includes luxury goods, of which the Young-Girl is certainly the most vulgar.

The Young-Girl never allows herself to be possessed as a Young-Girl in the same way that a commodity never allows itself to be possessed as a commodity, but only as a *thing*.

"YOU CAN BE PRETTY, SURROUNDED BY FRIENDS, PESTERED WITH PICK-UP LINES, AND YET ALONE INSIDE."

The Young-Girl only exists as a Young-Girl within the system of general equivalency and its massive circulatory movement. She is never possessed for the same reason that she is desired. The very moment one acquires her, she is taken out of circulation, the mirage fades, she sheds her magic aura and her nimbus of transcendence. She's stupid and she reeks.

> *"The modern world is not universally prostitutional for the sake of luxury. It would be incapable of that. It is universally prostitutional because it is universally interchangeable"* (Charles Péguy, *Note conjointe*).

The Young-Girl is the universal beneficiary of all the pseudo-concreteness of this world, and of the pseudo-objectivity of coitus first of all.

The Young-Girl would like to be a thing, but does not want to be treated like a thing. Yet all her distress comes not only from the fact that she's treated like a thing, but that on top of that she can't manage to really be a thing.

"No, my body is not a piece of merchandise. It's a tool for work."

The appalling thing isn't that the Young-Girl is fundamentally a whore, but that she refuses to perceive herself as such. Because the whore, being not only she who is bought, but also she who sells herself, is a maximalist figure of liberty among commodities.

The Young-Girl is a thing to the very extent that she takes herself to be human: She is a human being to the very extent that she takes herself to be a thing.

The whore represents the most eminent saintliness that the world of commodities can conceive of.

"Be yourself! (It pays.)"

One ruse of market thinking would have it appear that what she contains that is not on the order of commodities—what is "authentic" or "good" about her—determines the Young-Girl's value.

The Young-Girl is a crisis of coherence that shakes the very bowels of consumer society. She responds to the imperative of the total commodification of existence, to the necessity

of making sure nothing will remain outside the commodity form in what we still call, euphemistically, "human relations."

The mission she has been given is to re-enchant a devastated world of commodities, of prolonging the disaster with joy and insouciance. She inaugurates a form of second-degree consumption: the consumption of consumers. If we give credence to appearances, which has become legitimate in many cases, we would have to say that the commodity has achieved, through the Young-Girl, the total annexation of the non-commodity.

THE YOUNG-GIRL'S ASS REPRESENTS THE LAST BASTION OF ILLUSION OF A USE VALUE WHICH HAS SO MANIFESTLY DISAPPEARED FROM THE SURFACE OF EXISTENCE. THE IRONY, OF COURSE, IS THAT THIS VALUE IS STILL, ITSELF, AN *EXCHANGE*.

Within the Spectacle, we can say of the Young-Girl what Marx remarked about money, calling it "a special kind of commodity that is set apart from other commodities by a common act, and which serves to expose their reciprocal value."

5

THE YOUNG-GIRL AS LIVING CURRENCY

The Young-Girl becomes demonetized when she goes out of circulation. When she loses the possibility of re-entering the marketplace, she begins to rot.

The Young-Girl is the commodity specially assigned to the circulation of standard affects.

Value has never measured anything, but what it already failed to measure, it now measures more and more poorly.

Living money represents the ultimate answer of consumer society to the impotence of money to equal, and thus to purchase, the most notable human productions, those that are at once *the most precious and the most common.* For as the empire of money has spread to the farthest reaches of the world and to every expression of human life, it has lost all its specific value, it has become as impersonal as its concept, and consequently so negligible that its equivalency with anything personal has been rendered highly problematic. It is this absolute inequality between the empire of money and human life that has always shown itself in the impossible retribution of prostitution. With living money, market domination has been able to cancel these two impotencies—the one to purchase human life as such, which is to say, *power*, and the other, to purchase its most eminent productions—by multiplying them. Living money manages to render equivalent what is incommensurable in the personal creations of humanity—which have become preponderant—and what is incommensurable in human life. Henceforth, the Spectacle will estimate the inestimable via the inestimable in "objective" values.

"'Living currency': The industrial slave is both a sign guaranteeing wealth and the wealth itself. As a sign it stands for all manner of other material wealth, and as wealth it excludes all demands that are not those demands whose satisfaction it represents. But satisfaction proper is equally excluded by its being a sign" (Pierre Klossowski, *Living Currency*).

A quality of exclusion belongs to the Young-Girl, the Young-Girl as commodity, linked to the fact that she is *also*, irreducibly, a human being, which is to say something that is, like gold, a means to its own end. It is in light of this *exceptional* situation that she assumes the role of general equivalency.

Living currency, and specifically the Young-Girl, furnish a fairly plausible solution to the crisis of value, now incapable of measuring and remunerating those creations most characteristic of this society— those linked to the *general intellect.*

The conservation of minimal social conventions is conditioned by the fact that an excess of living currency would depreciate its value, rendering it incapable of constituting any real offset to the inestimable it is destined to purchase. At the same time, in rendering the inestimable estimable, it saps its own resources. The spectre of inflation haunts the world of Young-Girls.

The Young-Girl is the final cause *of spectacular economy and its prime mover, immobile.*

The Young-Girl's ass doesn't possess any new value, but only the unprecedented depreciation of all values that preceded it. The devastating power of the Young-Girl will have consisted in liquidating all products not convertible into living currency.

In this total nihilism, all notion of grandeur or prestige would have disappeared long ago, if they hadn't been immediately converted into Young-Girls.

The Young-Girl never misses a chance to extend the victory of living currency to mere money. Thus she requires, in exchange for herself, an infinite counter-gift.

Money has ceased to be the ultimate term of economy. Its triumph has depreciated it. The naked emperor, whose metaphysical content has deserted him, has also lost all value. Nobody in the biopolitical herd respects it anymore. Living currency is what has come to take the place of money as general equivalent, that *in light of which* its value is established. Living currency is its own value and concreteness. The purchasing power of living currency, and *a fortiori* of the Young-Girl, has no limits: It stretches to the totality of everything that exists, because in her, wealth enjoys itself doubly: both as sign and as fact. The high level of "individualization" of men and their creations, which had made money unfit to serve as mediator in purely personal relations, has now become the condition for the circulation of living currency.

It appears that all of the concreteness of the world has taken refuge in the ass of the Young-Girl.

Just as establishing social misery became necessary after '68 in order to return to commodities the honor they had lost, likewise sexual misery is necessary for the maintenance of the tyranny of the Young-Girl, of living currency. But the misery revealed here is no longer related to a temporal or economic context, on the contrary it is the essential misery of "sexuality" that has finally appeared.

"In the case of movables, possession gives title."

IN NO WAY DOES MONEY CONTRADICT LIVING CURRENCY. IT IS AN EARLIER MOMENT WHICH THE LATTER PRESERVES, WITH ALL OF ITS ACCOUNTING THAT NOW MEASURES NOTHING.

Once the translation of highly differentiated human life into money became impossible, THEY invented the Young-Girl, who restored to devalued money its value. But at the very same time she downgraded money, made it a secondary factor, the Young-Girl regenerated it, returning to it some substance. And it is thanks to this ruse that money survives.

The impersonality of the Young-Girl has the same ideal, impeccable, and purifying substance as money. The Young-Girl herself *has no smell*.

Just as "use value" bears no relation to its exchange value, the emotion that living money arouses is not susceptible to accounting and is not commensurate with any *thing*. But just as use value does not exist independent of exchange value, so the emotion aroused by living currency does not exist outside the system in which the latter is exchanged. One takes no more pleasure in the Young-Girl than one does in gold; one enjoys only their uselessness and scarcity. The indifference and insensitivity of Bloom were necessary preambles to concretizing the illusion of such an emotion, and its objectivity.

> When Marx posits that exchange value crystallizes the labor time that was necessary to produce the object, he affirms only that value is ultimately formed only by way of the life that has been canceled in the object, which is to say that living currency precedes all forms of cash.

"As soon as the corporeal presence of the industrial slave has fully entered the composition of the assessable output of what she can produce—her physiognomy being inseparable from her labor—the distinction between the person and the activity of that person becomes specious. The corporeal presence is already a commodity, independently of and in addition to the commodity this presence contributes to producing. Henceforth industrial slaves either establish an intimate relation between their corporeal presence and the money this presence brings in, or else they substitute themselves for the function of money, being money themselves: at once the equivalent of wealth and the wealth itself" (Pierre Klossowski, *Living Currency*).

In French, the verb "to fuck" is generically used to refer to any activity, though with a derogative connotation. "What the fuck are you doing?" And it is a reality that, in all societies in which man's activity is not free, *to fuck* occurs as freedom's general abstract equivalent, the degree zero of all activity.

It wasn't until the Young-Girl appeared that one could concretely experience what it means to "fuck," that is, to fuck someone without fucking anyone *in particular*. Because to fuck a being that is so really abstract, so utterly interchangeable, is to fuck in the absolute.

If money is the king of commodities, the Young-Girl is their queen.

THEY prefer silent pornstars—mute, without discourse—not because what pornstars have to say would be intolerable, or excessively crude, but on the contrary because, when they talk, what they say about themselves is nothing but the truth of all Young-Girls. "*I take vitamins to have nice hair,*" one of them confides. "*Taking care of your body is a daily job. It's normal, you have to work on your appearance, on the image people have of you.*"

In the final phase of the Spectacle, everything is sexually mediated, which is to say that coitus has been substituted as the ultimate goal of the utility of individual things. It is toward coitus that the existence of the world of the commodity now exclusively moves.

> *"As long as free love doesn't become widespread, a certain number of young girls will always be needed to fill the function that prostitutes fill today"* (Georg Simmel, *Philosophie de l'amour*).

Young-Girls in the service sector, marketing, retail, and social services. In a near and predictable future, all of the surplus value of the capitalist regime will be produced by Young-Girls.

The currency of coitus is self-esteem.

Every Young-Girl is an automatic, standard converter of existence into market value.

The Young-Girl is in fact neither the subject nor the object of emotion, but its *pretext*. One does not get off on a Young-Girl, or on her getting off; one gets off on getting off on her. A wager becomes necessary.

In many traditional cultures, money is the metaphor for woman, for fertility. In the time of the Young-Girl, woman becomes the metaphor of money.

Like money, the Young-Girl is the equivalent of herself, referring only to herself.

The Young-Girl is true gold, absolute cash.

It is a unilateral-fetishistic point of view that asserts that "the living object that is the source of emotion, from the point of view of exchange, is worth its maintenance cost" (Pierre Klossowski, *Living Currency*).

The time freed up by the increasing perfection and efficiency of the instruments of production did not result in any decrease in "labor" time, but in the extension of the sphere of "labor" into the totality of life, and especially in the constitution and maintenance of a sufficient stock of living currency, of *available* Blooms and Young-Girls, to give birth to a parallel and pre-regulated sexual marketplace.

The ghostly nature of the Young-Girl echoes the ghostly nature of participation in this society, for which the Young-Girl is also the remuneration.

Living money finally reveals the truth of commodity exchange, in other words, its lie: the impossibility of making equivalent the incommensurable in human life (classically coagulated in "labor time") and the inert, money, or any other *thing*, no matter what the quantity. For, in the end, the lie of market society has been to pass off what has always been a SACRIFICE as controlled exchange, and thus to claim to be settling an INFINITE DEBT.

6

THE YOUNG-GIRL AS COMPACT
POLITICAL APPARATUS

More distinctively, but no less fundamentally than a commodity, the Young-Girl constitutes an *offensive neutralization apparatus*.

How could capitalism have managed to mobilize affects, molecularizing its power to the point of colonizing all of our feelings and emotions, if the Young-Girl had not offered herself as *intermediary*? Like the economy, the Young-Girl thinks she's got us by the infrastructure.

Look on the bright side,
since History's happening on the dark side.
Biopower is available as a cream, pill, and spray.
Seduction is the new opium of the masses. It is the freedom of a world without freedom, the joy of a world without joy.

In the past, the terrifying example of a few liberated women was enough to convince the dominant powers of their chance to prohibit all feminine freedom.

By sentiment, by physiology, by family, by "sincerity," by "health," by wants, by obedience to all social determinisms, by all means, the Young-Girl protects herself from liberty.

> Behind the appearance of a laughable neutrality, the most formidable of political oppression apparatuses is on view in the Young-Girl.

"Is your sex life normal?"

The Young-Girl advances like a living engine, moved by and moving toward the Spectacle.

Domination has discovered a bias more powerful than the simple power of constraint: *directed attraction.*

The Young-Girl is the elementary biopolitical individuality.

Historically, the Young-Girl appears, in her extreme affinity with Biopower, as the spontaneous addressee of all biopolitics, the one whom THEY address.

> "EATING BADLY IS A LUXURY, A SIGN OF LAZINESS. DISDAIN FOR THE BODY IS A COMPLETELY COMPLACENT RELATION TO SELF. THE FEMALE WORKER MUST MAINTAIN HER BODY CAPITAL (GYM, POOL), WHILE FOR THE STUDENT, MORE IMPORTANT ARE AESTHETIC ACTIVITIES (DANCE) OR THE ULTIMATE PHYSICAL EXPENDITURE: THE NIGHTCLUB."

The function of the Young-Girl is to transform the promise of liberty contained in the achievement of Western civilization into a surplus of alienation, a deepening of the consumer order, new servitudes, a *political* status quo.

The Young-Girl advances toward the same endpoint as Technology: the formal spiritualization of the world.

Under the domination of the market, seduction immediately presents itself as the exercise of a *power*.

The Young-Girl has neither opinions nor positions of her own. She takes shelter as soon as she can in the shadow of the victors.

The "modern" kind of labor, in which a certain quantity of the labor force is no longer taken advantage of, but rather the docile exercise of certain "human qualities," suits perfectly well the mimetic skills of the Young-Girl.

The Young-Girl is the cornerstone of the system maintaining the market order, and is at the service of all its restorations. *Because the Young-Girl wants to fuck in peace.*

The Young-Girl is the ideal collaborator.

The Young-Girl conceives liberty as the possibility of choosing from among a thousand insignificances.

The Young-Girl *does not want history.*

The Young-Girl aims for *the regulation of all the senses.*

In the world of authoritarian commodities, all naive praise of desire immediately becomes praise of servitude.

There is no slave of semiocracy who does not also get a certain power out of it, the power of judgment, blame, or opinion.

The Young-Girl embodies the way in which capitalism has reinvested all of the necessities from which it had liberated men, reinvested them in an unrelenting adaptation of the human world to the abstract norms of the Spectacle, and in the elevation of these norms. Both share the morbid obsession of remaining, at the price of frantic activity, identical to themselves.

The narrow control and excessive solicitude displayed by this society toward women expresses only its desire to reproduce itself identically, and to **master** its perpetuation.

"The American Academy of Political and Social Sciences, in a publication on the role of women in modern America (1929), concluded that mass consumption had made of the 'modern housewife...less of a routine worker and more of an administrator and entrepreneur in the business of living'" (Stuart Ewen, *Captains of Consciousness: Advertising and the Social Roots of the Consumer Culture*).

The initial form of Biopower is a process of submission *to* and *by* the body.

The Spectacle keeps the body at bay through the excess of its evocation, just as religion evoked it by excessively prohibiting it.

The Young-Girl prizes "sincerity," "good-heartedness," "kindness," "simplicity," "frankness," "modesty," and in general all of the virtues which, considered unilaterally, are synonymous with servitude. The Young-Girl lives in the illusion that liberty is found at the end of total submission to market "Advertising." But at the end of servitude there is nothing but old age and death.

"LIBERTY DOESN'T EXIST," SAYS THE YOUNG-GIRL, WALKING INTO THE DRUGSTORE.

The Young-Girl wants to be "independent," that is, in her spirit, dependent on THEM alone.

Any grandeur that is not also a sign of subjugation to the world of authoritarian commodities is in that case consigned to the absolute detestation of the Young-Girl, who is not afraid to speak of "arrogance," "self-importance" and even "contempt."

The Young-Girl is the central article of permissive consumption and commodity leisure.

In the Spectacle, access to liberty is nothing but access to marginal consumption in the desire marketplace, which constitutes its symbolic core.

The preponderance of the entertainment and desire market is one stage in the project of social pacification, in which this market has been given the function of obscuring, provisionally, the living contradictions that traverse every point of the fabric of imperial biopolitics.

The symbolic privileges accorded by the Spectacle to the Young-Girl are her dividends for absorbing and diffusing the ephemeral codes, the updated user's manuals, the general semiology that THEY have had to dispense in order to render politically harmless the free time enabled by "progress" in the social organization of labor.

The Young-Girl:
the mainspring of "permissive discipline."

The Young-Girl: the agent coordinating the atmosphere and liveliness of the dictatorial management of leisure.

Deep down inside, the Young-Girl has the personality of a tampon: She exemplifies all of the appropriate indifference, all of the necessary coldness demanded by the conditions of metropolitan life.

It matters little to the Spectacle that seduction is hated everywhere, as long as people don't give themselves the idea that some plenitude could ever transcend it.

WHEN THE SPECTACLE ATTEMPTS TO "PRAISE FEMINITIY," OR REMARKS FAWNINGLY THE "FEMINIZATION OF THE WORLD," ONE CAN ONLY EXPECT THE CUNNING PROMOTION OF ALL MANNER OF SERVITUDES, THE PROMOTION OF THE CONSTELLATION OF "VALUES" THAT SLAVES ALWAYS PRETEND TO ESPOUSE.

"Ew! You're gross!"

The Young-Girl already represents the most effective agent of behavioral control. Through her, the dominant power has insinuated itself into the farthest reaches of everyone's life.

The violence with which femininitude is administrated in the world of authoritarian commodities recalls the way the dominant power feels free to manhandle its slaves, when in fact it needs them to ensure its own reproduction.

The Young-Girl is the power against which it is barbaric, indecent, and even downright totalitarian to rebel.

In the world of authoritarian commodities,
the living recognize within themselves,
in their alienated desires,
the enemy's demonstration of power.

7

THE YOUNG-GIRL AS WAR MACHINE

The Young-Girl displays spontaneous assent to everything that could possibly signify subjugation to necessity—"life," "society," "work," the education of a child, another Young-Girl. But this assent is itself determined in exclusively negative terms: Assent is given to these things only insofar as they block all individual expression.

There is always a penal colony hiding behind the Young-Girl's vitrified smile.

The Young-Girl knows no other legitimacy than that of the Spectacle. Inasmuch as the Young-Girl is docile under the arbitrary rule of THEM, she is tyrannical when it comes to the living. Her submission to the impersonality of the Spectacle gives her the right to submit anyone to it.

In fucking as in all other sectors of her existence, the Young-Girl behaves like a formidable mechanism for quashing negativity.

Because the Young-Girl is the living presence of everything that, humanely, wants our death. She is not only the purest product of the Spectacle, she is the plastic proof of our love for it. It is through her that we ourselves pursue our own perdition.

Everything she has managed to neutralize takes its place, in the world of the Young-Girl, as an **accessory**.
Seduction as war. THEY speak of "bombshells" using a metaphor derived less and less from aesthetic discourse, and more and more from that of ballistics.

Among the troops occupying all visibility, Young-Girls are the infantry, the rank-and-file of the current dictatorship of appearances.

The Young-Girl finds herself in a relationship of immediacy and affinity with everything that is competing to reformat humanity.

Every Young-Girl constitutes, in her own way, an advanced position in the imperialism of the trivial.

In terms of territory, the Young-Girl appears as the most powerful vector of the tyranny of servitude. Who can guess the fury enraging her at any sign of disobedience? In this sense, a certain type of totalitarian social democracy suits her marvelously.

The violence
of the Young-Girl
is proportional
to her delicate
emptiness.

It is through the Young-Girl that capitalism has managed to extend its hegemony to the totality of social life. She is the most obstinate pawn of market domination in a war whose objective remains the total control of daily life and "production" time.

It is precisely because she represents the total acculturation of the self, because she defines herself in terms fixed by extraneous judgment, that the Young-Girl constitutes the most advanced carrier of the *ethos* and the abstract behavioral norms of the Spectacle.

"One would have to create a major educational project (perhaps on the model of the Chinese or Khmer Rouge), with labor camps where boys would learn, under the direction of competent women, the responsibilities and secrets of domestic life."

The insignificance of the Young-Girl certainly reflects a situation of infantilization and oppression, yet she also has an imperialist and triumphant quality. This is because the Young-Girl fights for Empire, her master.

Unlike the young girls of Babylon, who, according to Strabo, willingly gave the temple the money they made from prostitution, the Young-Girl unwittingly turns her profits over to the Spectacle.

> "Furthermore, it was here that the schoolgirl's real pandemonium began: behind these letters there was a heap of confidential letters from judges, attorneys, public prosecutors, pharmacists, businessmen, urban and rural citizens, doctors and such, from those high and mighty who had always impressed me so! I stood there astonished [...] Did these men, pretense notwithstanding, socialize with the schoolgirl! 'Unbelievable,' I went on repeating, 'unbelievable!' Were they so oppressed by their Maturity that, unbeknownst to their wives and children, they had to send long letters to a modern schoolgirl? [...] These letters made me finally realize the extent of the schoolgirl's power. Where wasn't it present?" (Witold Gombrowicz, *Ferdydurke*)

The Young-Girl is a procedure of metaphysical sequestering, which is to say that one is never imprisoned *by* her, but always *in* her.

> The Young-Girl is a summons to everyone to ensure they are worthy of the images of the Spectacle.

The Young-Girl
is an instrument
in service to a general politics
of the extermination
of beings
capable
of love.

Identical in this
to the alienated social
whole,
the Young-Girl
hates sorrow
because sorrow
condemns her
*just as it condemns
this society.*

THE YOUNG-GIRL WORKS TO PROPAGATE
A TERRORISM OF ENTERTAINMENT.

—How many cops does it take to make a Young-Girl crack a childish smile?
—Even more, EVEN MORE,
          EVEN MORE…

The Young-Girl's vocabulary is also that of Total Mobilization.

"Loyalty, you'd better."

The Young-Girl is part of the new lifestyle-police, making sure that each person fulfills his or her *function*, and sticks exclusively to it. The Young-Girl *never* enters into contact with a singular being, but rather with a set of qualities objectivized in a role, a character, or a social situation to which one is supposed to conform no matter what the circumstance. Thus the person with whom she shares her own little alienated daily life will always remain "this guy" or "that girl."

The Young-Girl covets commodities with an eye filled with envy, because she sees her prototype in them, that is, she sees herself, only more perfect. What remains of her humanity is not only what she lacks in commodity perfection, it is also the cause of all her suffering. It is this remaining humanity, therefore, that she must eradicate.

With unfeigned bitterness the Young-Girl reproaches reality for failing to measure up to the Spectacle.

The ignorance with which the Young-Girl plays her role as cornerstone of the present system of domination *is part of the role*.

The Young-Girl is a pawn in the all-out war being waged by the dominant order for the eradication of all alterity. The Young-Girl declares it explicitly: She's "horrified by negativity." When she says this, she is, like Spinoza's stone, persuaded that it is she herself who is speaking.

The Young-Girl wears a mask, and, when she confesses to doing so, it is invariably to suggest that she also has a "true face" that she will not, or cannot, show. But this "true face" is still a mask, a terrifying mask: the true face of domination. Indeed, as soon as the Young-Girl "lets the mask fall," Empire is speaking to you *live*.

"... and what if we eliminated guys from the planet? Why try to get something new out of the old? Sick of guys? Get rid of them! No point getting annoyed—historically, genetically, man has done his time. He's leaving the stage all by himself."

Every Young-Girl is her own modest purification business.

Taken together, Young-Girls constitute the most lethal commando THEY have ever maneuvered against heterogeneity, against every hint of desertion. At the same time, they mark, at every instant, the most advanced position of Biopower, its poisonous solicitude, and its cybernetic pacification of everything. In the hungry gaze of the Young-Girl, each thing and each being, organic and inorganic, looks as though it could become possessed, or at least consumed. Everything she sees, she sees as and thus transforms into a commodity. It is in this sense that she also represents an advanced position in the infinite offensive of the Spectacle.

The Young-Girl is the void that THEY maintain in order to hide the vividness
o f   t h e   **v o i d** .

The Young-Girl doesn't like war, she makes it.

THE YOUNG-GIRL IS THE ULTIMATE SLAVERY THROUGH WHICH EMPIRE HAS OBTAINED ITS SLAVES' *SILENCE*.

It is not enough to know that the Young-Girl speaks the language of the Spectacle. It must be further noted that this is the only language she can understand, and that she thus requires all those who do not loathe it to speak it.

The semiocratic authorities, who demand ever more insistently an *aesthetic* assent to their world, pride themselves in their ability to pass off whatever they please as "beautiful." But this "beauty" is only socially controlled desire.

"SICK OF GUYS? GET A DOG! You're what, 18, 20? You're heading off to college to study long and hard? You think this is the time to lose your momentum by desperately looking for affection from a boy who's got nothing to give? Or worse! Get stuck with an undeveloped boyfriend who's not very mature, not very nice, and not always clean..."

The Young-Girl delivers conformity to all of the fleeting norms of the Spectacle, and also offers *the example* of such conformity.

Like everything that has achieved symbolic hegemony, the Young-Girl condemns as *barbaric* all physical violence directed against her aspiration of society's total pacification. She and the dominant power are obsessed with security.

The aspect of the war-machine so striking in every Young-Girl lies in the fact that she leads her life in a way no different from the way she wages war. But on the other hand, her pneumatic void already foreshadows her future militarization. She no longer defends only her private monopoly of desire, but in a general sense, the state of alienated public articulation of all desire.

It is not their "instinctive drives" that imprison people within the Spectacle, but the laws of what is desirable which THEY have inscribed into the flesh.

The Young-Girl has declared war on GERMS.
The Young-Girl has declared war on CHANCE.
The Young-Girl has declared war on PASSION.
The Young-Girl has declared war on TIME.
The Young-Girl has declared war on FAT.
The Young-Girl has declared war on OBSCURITY.
The Young-Girl has declared war on WORRY.
The Young-Girl has declared war on SILENCE.
The Young-Girl has declared war on POLITICS.

And finally,
THE YOUNG-GIRL HAS DECLARED WAR ON WAR.

8

THE YOUNG-GIRL AGAINST COMMUNISM

The Young-Girl privatizes everything she appre-
hends. Thus, a philosopher is not a philosopher
to her, but an extravagant erotic object, and likewise, a revolutionary is not a revolutionary, but
costume jewelry.

The Young-Girl is an article of consumption, a device for maintaining order, a
producer of sophisticated merchandise,
an unprecedented propagator of Spectacular
codes, an avant-garde of alienation,
and also, an entertainment.

**The *yes* that the Young-Girl says to life expresses
only her blind hate when faced with what is superior
to time.**

When the Young-Girl speaks of community, it is
always as a last resort the community of the species,
or of all living things, that she's thinking of it. She

never has a particular community in mind: after all, she would necessarily be excluded from it.

> **Even when she thinks she is engaging her whole "self" in a relationship, the Young-Girl is mistaken, because she fails to also engage her Nothingness. Thus, her dissatisfaction. Thus, her "friends."**

Because she discovers the world through the eyes of commodities, the Young-Girl sees in beings only what resembles commodities. Conversely, she considers the most personal in herself what is the most generic: coitus.

The Young-Girl wants to be loved for who she is, that is, for what isolates her. This is why she always maintains, in the very depths of her ass, *an evaluative distance.*

The Young-Girl epitomizes nothingness, the paradox, and of the tragedy of visibility.

> The Young-Girl is the privileged vehicle of socio-commodity Darwinism.

The continuous pursuit of sex is a manifestation of false substantiality. Its truth must not be sought in "pleasure," "hedonism," "the sexual instinct," or any other of the existential content Bloom has so definitively emptied of meaning, but rather in the frenzied search for some *connection* with a now inaccessible social whole. It is a matter, here, of giving oneself a feeling of *participation*, via the exercise of the most generic activity there is, the one that is most intimately linked to the reproduction of the species. This is the reason the Young-Girl is the most common and most sought-after object in this pursuit, because she is *the incarnation of the Spectacle*, or at least she aspires to be.

> To hear the Young-Girl talk, the question of *ultimate ends* becomes superfluous.

In a general sense, all false substantialities spontaneously earn the Young-Girl's favor. Some, however, are preferred by her. This goes for all of the pseudo-identities that can claim "biological" content (age, sex, height, race, menstruation, health, etc.).

The Young-Girl postulates an irrevocable intimacy with everything that shares her physiology. Her function is thus to maintain the dying flame of the illusions of immediacy upon which Biopower comes to depend.

The Young-Girl is the termite of the "material," the marathon runner of the "everyday." Domination has made her into the privileged carrier of the ideology of the "concrete." Not only does she thrive on "easy," "simple," "real life"; but she also considers the "abstract," the "hassle," as evils it would be judicious to eradicate. Yet what she calls the "concrete" is itself, in its savage unilateralism, the most abstract. It is the shield of wilted flowers hiding the progress of that for which she has been conceived: the violent negation of metaphysics. Not only does she resent what she doesn't understand, it infuriates her. Her hatred for what is great, for what is beyond the grasp of the consumer, is immeasurable.

The Young-Girl uses the "concrete" to keep herself from succumbing to the metaphysical feeling of her nothingness.

"Evil is whatever distracts" (Kafka).

In truth, the "love of life" on which the Young-Girl prides herself is nothing but her hatred of danger. Her pride thus only reveals her determination to maintain immediacy with what she calls "life"; which, more precisely, means "life in the Spectacle."

Among all the aporias whose pretentious accumulation constitutes Western metaphysics, the most durable seems to be the formation, by repudiation, of a sphere of "bare life." There is supposed to be, beyond qualified—political, presentable—human existence, an abject, indistinct, unqualifiable sphere of "bare life": reproduction, domestic economy, the maintenance of vital faculties, heterosexual *coupling*, or food, all things that THEY have associated, as much as possible, with "feminine identity," converging in this primordial swamp. Young-Girls have only redirected the signs of an operation that they have left otherwise unchanged. It is thus that they have forged a very curious species of commonality which THEY would call the being-for-life, if THEY knew that the common point of Western metaphysics had been belatedly identified as the being-for-death. So much so that Young-Girls have become persuaded that they are united most profoundly by physiology, daily life, psychology, bedroom gossip, and THEM. The repeated failure of their love affairs, like their friendships, seems incapable of opening their eyes, nor can it make them see that that is precisely what keeps them apart.

Against finitude, the Young-Girl opposes the groaning of her organs. Against solitude, the continuity of the living. And against the tragedy of exposure, the sense that it's good to get noticed.

Like the beings that constitute its terms, the relationships that develop in the Spectacle are deprived both of content and meaning. If only the lack of meaning, so obvious throughout the Young-Girl's life drove her insane; but no, it only leaves her in her state of terminal nonsense. The establishment of these terms is not dictated by actual usage—strictly speaking, Young-Girls have nothing to *do* together—nor is it dictated by their taste, however unilateral, for one another—even their tastes do not belong to them—but by symbolic utility alone, which makes each partner a *sign* of the *happiness* of the other, the paradisiac completeness that it is the Spectacle's aim to continuously redefine.

Naturally, it is by becoming an argument for Total Mobilization that seduction has taken the form of the job interview and "love" a kind of mutual, private employment—with job security for the lucky ones.

"Don't worry!"

THE YOUNG-GIRL PUNISHES NO BETRAYAL MORE SEVERELY THAN THAT OF THE YOUNG-GIRL WHO DESERTS THE CORPS OF YOUNG-GIRLS, OR EVEN ATTEMPTS TO FREE HERSELF FROM IT.

The Young-Girl's essential activity not only consists in separating the "professional" from the "personal," the "social" from the "private," the "emotional" from the "useful," the "reasonable" from the "crazy," the "everyday" from the "exceptional," etc., but above all of embodying these distinctions in her "life."

The Young-Girl can well speak of death; she will invariably conclude that after all,

"that's life."

The Young-Girl "loves life," which really means that she hates all *forms-of-life*.

The Young-Girl is like everything that speaks of "love" in a society that does everything to render it utterly impossible: She lies in the name of domination.
What the Young-Girl's "youth" designates is nothing but a certain obstinacy in negating finitude.

The Young-Girl's ass is a global village.

When she speaks of "peace" and "happiness," the Young-Girl's face is that of death. Her negativity is not of the spirit, but of the inert.

The Young-Girl possesses a singular connection to bare life, in all its *forms*.

The Young-Girl has entirely rewritten the book of deadly sins. On the first page, she has written, in cute calligraphy,

"Solitude."

The Young-Girl swims holding her breath through immanence.

9

THE YOUNG-GIRL AGAINST HERSELF:
THE YOUNG-GIRL AS IMPOSSIBILITY

That the Spectacle would have finally reached the absurd metaphysical conception according to which everything is supposed to issue from its Idea and not the opposite—this is a superficial view. In the Young-Girl, we clearly see just how THEY obtain a reality such that it seems to be nothing but the materialization of its concept: THEY amputate it from everything that would make it singular to the point of making it similar *in poverty* to an idea.

This *human* foreignness to the world of commodities relentlessly pursues the Young-Girl and constitutes, for her, the supreme menace, *"menace that, factually, is in no way incompatible with complete security and the complete absence of need in the order of everyday preoccupation"* (Martin Heidegger). This anguish, which is the fundamental mode of being of whosoever can no longer *inhabit* his or her world, is the central, universal, and *hidden* truth of the era of the Young-Girl, and of the Young-Girl herself: hidden, because it is when she is shut away at home, far from any gaze, that she sobs and sobs. For she who is gnawed by nothingness, this anguish is the other name for the solitude, the silence, and dissimulation that are her metaphysical condition, which she has such a hard time getting used to.

For the Young-Girl as for all other Blooms, the craving for entertainment is rooted in anguish.

Sometimes the Young-Girl is bare life, and sometimes she is death dressed up. In fact, she is that which *constantly* holds both together.

The Young-Girl is closed up on herself;

this fascinates at first,

and then it begins to rot.

ANOREXIA IS INTERPRETED AS A FANATICISM OF DETACHMENT THAT, GIVEN THE IMPOSSIBILITY OF ANY METAPHYSICAL PARTICIPATION IN THE WORLD OF COMMODITIES, SEEKS ACCESS TO A *PHYSICAL* PARTICIPATION IN IT, WHICH, OF COURSE, FAILS.

"Spirituality: our new need? Is there a hidden mystic in all of us?"

Self-interest is but the apparent motive of the Young-Girl's behavior. In the act of selling herself, she is trying to acquit herself of herself, or at least have THEM acquit her. But this never happens.

Anorexia expresses in women the same aporia that is manifest in men in the form of the pursuit of power: the will to mastery. It is only that, because of the greater severity of the culture's patriarchal codification upon women, the anorexic brings the will to mastery to bear upon her body, for she cannot bring it to bear on the rest of the world. A pandemic similar to the one we see today among Young-Girls emerged at the heart of the Middle Ages among the saints. Against the world that would reduce her to her body, the Young-Girl opposes her sovereignty over her body. In the same way, the saint opposed the patriarchal mediation of the clergy to her own direct communion with God; she opposed the dependency through which THEY would have liked to keep her to her radical independence from the world. In saintly anorexia, "the suppression of physical urges and basic feelings—fatigue, sexual drive, hunger, pain—frees the body to achieve heroic feats and the soul to commune with God" (Rudolph Bell, *Holy Anorexia*).

Now that the medical profession has replaced the clergy in the patriarchal order as well as at the bedside of the anorexic Young-Girl, the cure rates for what THEY have rapidly named "anorexia nervosa" are still exceptionally low, in spite of considerable therapeutic perseverance here as elsewhere; only in a few countries has the mortality rate fallen below 15%. For the death of the anorexic, whether she is holy or "mental," only sanctions her final victory over her body, over the world. As in the intoxication of a hunger strike pushed to the end, the Young-Girl finds in death the ultimate affirmation of her detachment and purity. "[…] the anorexics struggle against feeling enslaved, exploited, and not being permitted to lead a life of their own. They would rather starve than continue a life of accommodation. In this blind search for a sense of identity and selfhood, they will not accept anything that their parents or the world around them has to offer. [… In what] I shall refer to as genuine or primary anorexia nervosa, the main issue is a struggle for control, for a sense of identity, competence and effectiveness" (Hilde Bruch, *Eating Disorders: Obesity, Anorexia Nervosa, and the Person Within*).

"*Indeed,*" concludes the postscript to *Holy Anorexia*, "*anorexia could be seen as a tragic caricature of the disconnected, self-sufficient female, unable to affiliate and driven by an obsessive desire for power and mastery.*"

There is indeed an objectivity of the Young-Girl, but it is an imaginary objectivity. She is a contradiction frozen in tomblike immobility.

Whatever she says, it is not the right to happiness that the Young-Girl is denied, but the right to unhappiness.

Whatever the happiness of the Young-Girl might be in each of the separated aspects of her existence (work, love, sex, leisure, health, etc.), she must remain essentially unhappy *precisely because these aspects are separated*.

Unhappiness is the fundamental mood of the existence of the Young-Girl.
This is good.
Unhappiness makes people consume.

The suffering and unhappiness intrinsic to the Young-Girl demonstrate the impossibility of any end of History in which men would content themselves with being the most intelligent of the animal species, renouncing all discursive consciousness, all desire for recognition, any exercise of their negativity, the impossibility, in a word, of *the American way of life*.

When she hears talk of negativity, the Young-Girl calls her therapist. She has all kinds of words to avoid talking about metaphysics when it has the bad taste to make itself heard too distinctly: "psychosomatic" is one of them.

Like the model that she has necessarily, at one moment or another, dreamed of becoming, the Young-Girl aims at total inexpressivity, at ecstatic absence, but the image has been sullied by its incarnation, and the Young-Girl manages only to express the void, the living void, seething and oozing, the humid void—until she vomits.

The cyborg as supreme and immunodeficient stage of the Young-Girl.

The Young-Girl gets depressed because she would like to be a thing *like other things*, that is, like other things *seen from outside*, though she can never quite manage it; because she would like to be a sign, to circulate without friction through the gigantic semiocratic metabolism.

The whole life of the Young-Girl coincides with what she wants to forget.

The apparent sovereignty of the Young-Girl is also the absolute vulnerability of the separated individual, the weakness and isolation that nowhere find either the shelter, security, or protection they seem to be seeking everywhere. Indeed, the Young-Girl lives forever "hot on her own tail," that is, in *fear*.

The Young-Girl presents us with the authentic *enigma* of *happy servitude,* in which we are not quite able to believe. The mystery of the radiant slave.

The pursuit of happiness summarizes, as its effect but also as its *cause*, the unhappiness of the Young-Girl. The Young-Girl's frenzy over appearances manifests her craving for substance that can find nothing on which to slake itself.

All the elegance of the Young-Girl never manages to make one forget her invincible vulgarity.

"Everybody beautiful, everything organic!"

The Young-Girl wants the *best of all worlds*. Unfortunately the "best of all worlds" *is not possible*.
The Young-Girl dreams of a body that would be purely transparent to the lights of the Spectacle. In all, she dreams of being nothing more than the idea THEY have of her.
Frigidity is the truth of nymphomania, impotence is the truth of Don Juan, anorexia is the truth of bulimia.

Because in the Spectacle, where the appearance of happiness also functions as its *sine qua non* condition, the duty to simulate happiness is the way to all suffering.
The translucent nonexistence of the Young-Girl attests to the false transcendence she personifies.

What the Young-Girl demonstrates is that no beautiful surface is without its terrible depth.

The Young-Girl is the emblem of an existential anguish expressed in the unfounded feeling of permanent insecurity.

The Spectacle consents to speak of sexual misery, in order to stigmatize people's incapacity to exchange one another like perfect commodities. It is true that the obstinate imperfection of the marketplace of seduction is worrying.

The anorexic scorns the things of this world in the only way that makes her more contemptible than they are.

Like so many other of our unhappy contemporaries, the Young-Girl has taken the aporias of Western metaphysics literally. And it is in vain that she seeks to give herself *form* as bare life.

The extreme extent
of male
impotence, of
female frigidity
or rather
of vaginal dryness
can be interpreted
immediately as
contradictions
of capitalism.

Anorexia expresses, at the level of the commodity, the most incontinent disgust for them, and for the vulgarity of all wealth. In all of her bodily manifestations, the Young-Girl signifies an impatient rage to abolish matter and time. She is a body without soul dreaming she's a soul without a body.

> *"[…] the onset of Saint Catherine of Siena's anorexia was a consequence […] of psychic factors, in her case her will to conquer bodily urges that she considered base obstructions in her path of holiness"* (Rudolph Bell, *Holy Anorexia*).

In anorexia, we must see much more than a fashionable pathology: the desire to free oneself from a body entirely colonized by commodity symbolism, to reduce to nothing a physical objectivity the Young-Girl wholly lacks.

But this leads, finally, only in her making a new body from the negation of the body.

IN THE ANOREXIC YOUNG-GIRL, AS IN THE ASCETIC IDEAL, THE SAME HATRED OF THE FLESH, AND THE FANTASY OF REDUCING ONESELF TO PHYSICAL PURITY: THE SKELETON.

The Young-Girl suffers from what we could call the "angel complex": She aspires to a perfection that would consist in having *no body*. She can read the unilateralism of commodity metaphysics whenever she steps onto a scale.

The anorexic seeks the absolute in her own way, that is, she seeks the worst of absolutes in the worst way.

Bloom's desire, and consequently the Young-Girl's, is not for bodies, but for essences.

The absolute vulnerability of the Young-Girl is that of the shopkeeper, whose merchandise can be stolen by any uncontrollable force.

The Young-Girl is a "metaphysical" creature in the adulterated, modern sense of the term. She would not submit her body to such ordeals, to such cruel penance, if she weren't fighting against it as though it were the devil himself, if she didn't yearn to submit it entirely to *form*, to the ideal, to the dead perfection of abstraction. This metaphysics is ultimately nothing but the hatred of the physical, conceived here as simply the other side of metaphysics.

"HOW TO DRESS ORGANICALLY."

The Young-Girl is the commodity's ultimate attempt at transcending itself. It fails miserably.

10

PUTTING AN END TO THE YOUNG-GIRL

The Young-Girl is a reality as massive and crumbly as the Spectacle.

Like all transitory forms, the Young-Girl is an oxymoron. She is thus the first case of asceticism without ideal, of materialist penance.

Cowardly devoted to the whims of the Young-Girl, we have learned to disdain her while obeying her.
The sexual misery of today in no way resembles that of the past, because it is now bodies without desires that burn for not being able to satisfy them.

In the course of its metastasized development, seduction has lost in intensity what it has gained by extension. Never has amorous discourse been so poor as when everyone made it their duty to intone it and comment upon it.

The Young-Girl does not have the face of a dead girl, as one might think from reading avant-garde women's magazines, but of death itself.

Everyone seeks to sell him or herself, but nobody manages to do so convincingly. Contrary to what might seem to be happening, at first glance, the rapist does not struggle with a particular woman or man, but with *sexuality itself*, as an authority of control.

Upon its emergence, the naked body of the Young-Girl succeeded in producing a sense of truth. Since then, we have vainly sought such a power in ever *younger* bodies.

The charms we no longer find in the Young-Girl are the exact measure of what we have already managed to liquidate in her.

The question is not of the emancipation of the Young-Girl, but of emancipation *in relation* to the Young-Girl.

In certain extreme cases, one sees the Young-Girl turning the void within her against the world that made her what she is. The pure void of her form, her profound hostility to everything that is, will condense into explosive blocs of negativity. She will have to ravage everything that surrounds her. The barren expanse that substitutes for interiority will long to reduce some stretch of Empire to equivalent desolation. "*Give me a bomb, I have to die,*" exalted a Russian nihilist in the last century, begging to be given the suicide attack on Grand-Duke Sergei.

For the Young-Girl, as for a man in power, who in every way resemble each other when they don't simply coincide, de-subjectivation cannot avoid a collapse, a collapse *in oneself.* Differences in the height of the fall simply measure the gulf between the fullness of social being and the extreme anemia of singular being; in other words, finally, the poverty of the relation to the self. And yet, there is, in the one's destitution, the *power* that lacks in the completeness of the other.

"But I had to remove the aura in which man looks to wreathe this other female figure, the apparently immaterial young girl deprived of sensuality, by showing that she is precisely the same kind of mother, and that virginity is, by definition, as foreign to her as to a courtesan. Indeed, the study also shows that maternal love itself has no moral value attached to it" (Otto Weininger, *Sex and Character*).

Rarely has an epoch been so violently shaken by desires, and rarely has desire been so *empty.*

The Young-Girl makes one think of the monumentality of platonic architecture looming over the present; it gives only a fleeting idea of eternity, for it is already cracking. Occasionally the Young-Girl also makes one think of something else: a hovel, invariably.

"I COULD DESTROY THE SCHOOLGIRL'S MODERNITY BY INTRODUCING INTO IT FOREIGN AND HETEROGENEOUS ELEMENTS, SCRAMBLING EVERYTHING UP FOR ALL IT WAS WORTH" (WITOLD GOMBROWICZ, *FERDYDURKE*).

Beneath the apparent disorder of the desires of the Caserne Babylone *the order of self-interest* reigns supreme. But the order of self-interest itself is only a secondary reality, whose justification does not lie in itself, but in the desire for desire found at the foundation of every *failed* life.

Changes in the Young-Girl symmetrically follow the evolution of capitalist modes of production. Thus, over the past thirty years, we have passed, little by little, from Fordist seduction, with its designated sites and moments, its static and proto-bourgeois couple-form, to post-Fordist seduction, diffuse, flexible, precarious and deritualized, which has extended the couple factory to the entire body and the whole of social time-space. At this particularly advanced stage of Total Mobilization, each of us is called on to maintain our "seduction power," the substitute for "labor power," such that, on the sexual marketplace, we can be fired and rehired at any moment.

The Young-Girl mortifies her flesh in order to take revenge on Biopower and the symbolic violence to which the Spectacle subjects it.

The distress she exhibits overwhelmingly reveals, in its former aspect of unshakeable positivity, sexual pleasure as the most metaphysical of physical pleasures.

"Some make sophisticated, hip, 'trendy' magazines. We've made a healthy magazine: fresh, airy, filled with blue skies and organic fields, a magazine more authentic than nature itself."

THE YOUNG-GIRL IS ENTIRELY CONSTRUCTED. THIS IS WHY SHE CAN ALSO BE ENTIRELY DESTROYED.

It is only in her suffering that the Young-Girl is lovable. There is, evidently, a subversive power in trauma.

The success of the mimetic logic that has carried the Young-Girl to her present triumph also contains the necessity of her extinction.

It is finally the inflation of Young-Girls that will have most surely undermined the efficacy of each of them.

The theory of the Young-Girl participates in the training of a gaze that knows how to hate the Spectacle wherever it hides, that is, wherever it shows itself.

Who, aside from a few halfwit stragglers, can still be seriously moved in the face of *"the ruse, the device by which he knows how to insinuate himself into the heart of the Young-Girl, the influence he knows how to hold over her, finally, the fascinating, calculated, and methodical character of seduction"* (Søren Kierkegaard)?

Wherever the commodity is unloved, so is the Young-Girl.

The spread of the seduction relation into all social activities signals the death of whatever was still living within it. The spread of simulation is also what renders seduction more and more obviously impossible. Now is the time of the greatest unhappiness, the streets filled with heartless sensualists, seducers mourning for seduction, the corpses of desires nobody knows what to do with. It would be a physical phenomenon, like a loss of aura. As though the electrification of bodies, an intense separation had caused, began to spread to the point of disappearance. Out of this, a new proximity would emerge, and new distances.

A total exhaustion of desire would mean the end of the market society and, for that matter, of all society.

Landscape of a ravaged eros

"As a general thesis, social progress and changes in time periods occur because of the progress of women toward liberty" (François Marie Charles Fourier).

When the Young-Girl has exhausted all artifice, there is one final artifice left for her: the renunciation of artifice. But this last one *really* is the final one.

In making itself the Trojan Horse of worldwide domination, desire has emptied itself of everything that smacked of domesticity, cosiness, privacy. The precondition of totalitarian reconfiguration of what is desirable has been its autonomy from every real object and all particular content. In learning to train itself on essences, desire has become, despite itself, an absolute desire, a desire for the absolute that nothing earthly can quench.

This unquenchability is the central lever of consumption, and of its subversion.

A communization of bodies is to be expected.

Does the everyday occurrence of the Young-Girl still go without saying?

The Young-Girl is currently the most luxurious of the goods that circulate on the market of perishable commodities,

the beacon-commodity of the fifth industrial revolution which enables the sale of all the others, from life insurance to nuclear

power, the monstrous and very real dream of the most intrepid the most fantastical of retailers:

autonomous commodities that walk, talk, and silence, *the thing that is finally alive*, that no longer seizes life, but digests it.

Three thousand years of tireless labor by thousands of plump shopkeepers,

generation after generation finding their crowning achievement in the Young-Girl: for she is the *commodity one is forbidden to burn*, the stock that engenders itself, the inalienable and

nontransferable property for which one must still pay, the virtue that relentlessly makes money; she is the slut who *demands*

espect, death roiling in itself, she is the law and the police at he same time... Who has not, in a flash, seen in her decisive nd funereal beauty the sex appeal of the inorganic?

semiotext(e) intervention series